Sins of Omission

Things Your Broker Should Be Telling You!

Mike Kaselnak

ISBN 0-9745175-1-8

This publication is written to provide acurate and authoritative information in regard to the subject matter covered. It is distributed with the understanding that the publisher and author are not engaged in rendering legal, accounting, or other professional services. If legal advice or other expert assistance is required, the services of a competent professional should be sought.

Chapter   Contents

A Lifetime of Experience

I began investing in the stock market as a senior in high school, but it wasn't until I'd been in the Navy for six years and had been through Corporate America before I finally decided to tie my vocation to my love of investing. In 1989, I landed my first job as a stockbroker with IDS Financial Services, which is now American Express Financial Corporation.

Within three-and-a-half months of joining IDS, I had become one of the top financial planning salespeople in Minnesota, and over the next two years I sold a lot of financial plans to people. But along the way I learned something about the business of financial planning.

I was becoming conflicted between my job and my clients. While I truly believed in the planning services I provided, I felt uncomfortable with the products I offered. It wasn't that the products were bad, but I was handcuffed because I could only sell American Express products. Having already spent 15 years investing on my own, I knew there was a lot more to investing than a handful of products, and shortly thereafter my business began to drop.

In early 1991 things came to a head when my manager yelled at me for reading the *Wall Street Journal.* I was told that, despite the newspaper's popularity, it "was not approved reading mater-ial for American Express brokers."

At that moment, it became clear to me that my suspicions about the business were correct. My manager didn't want me to read the *Wall Street Journal* because I might learn about other prod-ucts we didn't offer. After all, why would anyone discourage a stockbroker from reading such an important financial newspaper? Shouldn't brokers be encouraged to broaden their exposure to the financial world?

Within two weeks of that incident, I quit my job at IDS and became an independent broker. About a year later I gave another brokerage firm a try when I was recruited by Norwest, which is now part of Wells Fargo Bank. At the time, they were beginning their investment services through branches of their bank. So rather than have clients come to my office, I traveled from branch to branch selling products and helping people all over Southeastern Minnesota. On Monday I might be around the corner from my home, but Tuesday I'd be 40 miles away, and by Wednesday I'd be almost a hundred miles away from home.

As you might imagine, my business was very transaction-ori-ented to say the least. The system was set up in such a way that I was expected to sell stocks, bonds, and mutual funds on an as-needed basis, which meant that I saw someone one time and told them which product they needed. With so much traveling, it was next to impossible to encourage and build long-term relationships with my clients.

So as with IDS, I became frustrated with the idea of being just a financial salesman and left two-and-a-half years later because of the constant stress of meeting sales quotas and hour upon hour behind the wheel of my car. When I left, I had close to nine hundred clients, yet I barely knew any of the people I was servicing. I knew in my heart that I wasn't really helping people as much as selling things for commission.

From there, I went back to being an independent advisor and earned my CFP® designation. A CFP® is a Certified Financial Planner, which is an independent third-party designation that brokers and advisors voluntarily receive to indicate their knowledge about financial planning and its ethical considerations. In order to earn my CFP® designation, I had to go through a comprehensive program of classes and tests, as well as take continuing education classes on a regular basis.

About three years into my second stint as an independent advisor, I had an epiphany. One night I was sitting at my dining room table reviewing stacks of financial information and records about my clients, and I was getting frustrated. At the time, I was subscribing to lots of financial newsletters, publications, and other investment programs to make sure I was a well-rounded and knowledgeable advisor. Yet despite my library of financial knowledge, I was pulling my hair out. Before long I was swearing, cursing, and banging my fist on the table in anger.

"What's wrong with you?" my wife asked as she entered the room. "What are you doing?"

"Here, look at this," I said as I shoved a notepad in her face. "Over the last three years I've invested $30,000 in different investment systems, newsletter subscriptions, and strategies, but if I had just taken that $30,000 and put it in the bank at 3% interest, I would have made more money than by using these systems!"

I should take a moment to explain my investment strategy as

an advisor. I'd read and learn about various systems of investing, but before I'd ever put a dime of my clients' money into them, I'd research them for years to make sure they actually worked. But every time I became convinced that I was doing the right thing, I'd put my clients' money into them and – you guessed it – they'd stop working.

I was understandably frustrated with myself and took the opportunity to make a point to my wife. "You know what?" I told her, "If I had just put that $30,000 in the S&P 500, I would have beaten everything else I've tried without even using my brain."

And my wonderful wife, who's a psychologist at the Mayo Clinic, asked me a question that changed my life.

"So why can't you just invest in the S&P 500?"

At that moment my whole world went black. In three seconds my wife had said something that I had known for years, but couldn't admit to myself. Yet once I heard it, I knew she was right.

Yes, I could invest my clients' money in the S&P 500. And yes, that was the best place to invest. But if I encouraged people to invest in the S&P 500, I wouldn't make any money. People could do that without me with no commission or help.

At the time, exchange traded funds, which are mutual funds that can be traded during market hours like stocks, didn't exist, so the best option was to use Vanguard, a no-load, low-cost mutual fund, and invest everything in the fund straight into the S&P 500. But I wanted to be honest with my clients, which meant if I did that with my own personal money, I'd have to recommend that my clients do the same.

I was faced with a difficult decision. The way I saw it I had three choices. Number one was that I could be unethical by doing what was right for me, which was investing in the S&P 500, and recommend my clients invest in managed funds, mutual funds, and variable annuities so I could earn a commission. There was no way I would be able to do that and live with myself.

Number two was to continue to invest in the same actively managed funds that my clients owned, which meant both making less money on my investments with more risk, and my clients making less in their investments, all for the sake of a commission from my client. That would be just poor business sense.

Number three was to encourage my clients to invest in the S&P 500, and I would do the same. Sure, I'd be able to sleep at night, but my business would go broke.

So the best I could tell, I was out of business. I wasn't going to have my clients do something that I wouldn't do myself. I certainly didn't want to be putting my own money into poor investments, and being broke was not an option. I was about to give up.

But at that point something happened. This was 1996, and a technique had been invented that gave people the ability to invest in the index while utilizing a guaranteed or insured blanket around it. This meant that I could encourage my clients to do what I thought was best, which was to invest in indexes such as the S&P 500, but that I could also get compensated by helping them protect their investments if the market went down.

Also around this time, a family member of mine had gone into a long-term care facility. Because I was an advisor and a CFP®, my family came to me and asked for help with my relative's financial situation. After all, I'm supposed to be an expert on finances, right?

But what I found out was that I didn't know the least bit about seniors and long-term care. So I consulted some other advisors for their advice, and they knew just enough to be dangerous. Then I consulted some attorneys for their advice, and they also knew just enough to be dangerous. Then I consulted my accountant, and like everyone else, he knew just enough to be dangerous. So while everyone had a few ideas of what to do, no one was able to see the big picture and address everything that was involved.

As I struggled to help my family, a light bulb went on. Without realizing it, I had stumbled onto a group of individuals whose financial needs were not being addressed and serviced. And it wasn't because no one wanted to help them; the problem was that professionals like myself didn't know what was needed or how to help them.

Shortly thereafter, I revised my practice and began working solely with senior investors. I had about 350 clients at the time and kept the 35 who were 55 or older. The rest I visited individually, told them what I was doing, and set them up with other brokers in my town.

One of the things I did to build my business and help senior investors during this time was to hold workshops that would help them. And as I began doing this, I found that there was a great need for someone who understood the financial needs of seniors and their unique situations.

Over the next seven years, I continued my business, helping seniors and holding workshops to educate them. As things progressed, I became very well known throughout Minnesota as the best advisor for seniors and retired individuals because of my experience in this area.

Why I Left the Business

My business continued successfully until 2002, and during these seven years, I slowly began to realize that although many brokers and advisors were serving senior investors, they were not always doing what was best for the client. Some financial professionals ignored important issues that seniors need to address, while others were more concerned with selling products to senior investors than doing financial planning for them. I started spending more and more time specifically addressing all the things other advisors forget which, unfortunately, was a significant portion of what seniors needed to protect themselves and their families.

I learned that the vast majority of advisors and brokers knew very little about what retired individuals actually needed. And because of this lack of experience, many clients in my area left their advisors and asked me to help them with their financial affairs.

It wasn't long before many of my fellow brokers and advisors complained about me. In fact, some of them complained to the Certified Financial Planner Board of Standards, the organization responsible for the CFP® designation.

When problems arose between the board of Certified Financial Planners and me, the board set up a phone appointment to discuss the situation. During the meeting, I was chastised for taking clients away from fellow professionals. I responded by insisting that I would never pull clients away from another financial professional.

"You're doing it on a regular basis," the board told me. "You're pulling approximately a hundred clients away from professionals in your area every single year."

I insisted that this wasn't the case. "What do you mean?" they asked me as they started naming names of brokers that had lost clients to me.

"That's my point," I said. "They left their brokers to come to me because they weren't acting like financial professionals. Shouldn't financial professionals help their clients make sure they have the correct beneficiaries on all their investments? Shouldn't they be helping clients reduce their taxes as much as legally possible? Shouldn't they be making sure that their clients are getting the highest return possible with the least amount of risk?"

Once the board agreed with my questions, I explained myself. "Well, none of these people came to me because of a product that I offer. They left their advisors and came to me because I was handling things other brokers either didn't know how to do or didn't want to take the time to do."

By the end of our meeting, I was unable to get the CFP Board to understand my position, so we agreed to disagree and left the matter at that.

Less than two months later, I saw that Suze Orman, the well-known financial author, columnist, and guru, was basically having the same problem with the CFP Board. Suze, a CFP$^®$ like myself, was being threatened with discipline for using what the board considered to be derisive language about brokers.

Yet Suze was doing much the same thing I was, which was saying that clients need to work with someone who cares about them, not someone who's concerned about the size of their commission check. And Suze emphasized that selling a product does not demonstrate caring. Selling a product demonstrates that someone cares about their own pocketbook, rather than their client.

So after a year of watching the investment world deteriorate and continue to ignore the needs of investors, I decided to leave the business. The CFP Board had begun allowing a few firms to give their brokers abbreviated versions of the CFP® designation, and many members left in anger at what they considered to be a deterioration in the ideals behind the designation.

I was one of those members, and I decided to retire my CFP® designation because I believe their actions were not in the best interests of clients or the profession. This was the same time that Wall Street greed and fraud became daily news across the country. There were fraud issues with several mutual fund companies, corporate executives like Dennis Kozlowski of Tyco were on trial for stealing corporate funds, and investor confidence in the financial industry and corporate executives was at an all-time low.

I was angry and disappointed with what the financial services industry had become and decided that the best thing I could do was to leave the industry and use my knowledge to help senior investors like yourself protect their years of hard work and effort.

I hope you'll agree that I made the right decision.

About the Handbook

B uilding upon my experience, I've written this book to help you, the senior investor, learn what your financial advisor should be doing to look out for your best interests. Whether it's IRAs, long-term care insurance, or setting up estates, you need to know what to expect from your advisor. And if this book teaches you that your current advisor isn't giving you the help you deserve, I'll teach you how to find one who will.

But it's important to remember one thing. You should never act on the ideas in this book alone, and I can't emphasize this enough. This book is designed to help find the best advisor for you, not to replace your advisor. In absolutely no way am I suggesting that you fire your advisor if he or she has been doing his or her job, or that you start handling your investments alone. Being your own advisor is great, but anyone who does so must hold him or herself to the same standards as a professional. So don't put these ideas to use before you consult with a competent advisor who specializes in working with seniors.

In fact, if you come across something that you want to know more about or need to fix in your own portfolio, make a note of it and call an advisor. Run these ideas by him or her, and get his or her advice. Be sure to ask questions and decide for yourself if his or her advice is appropriate for you.

Above all, I want this book to help you become an informed consumer, and it will be a valuable resource as you and a qualified senior advisor work to improve your financial situation.

The Senior's Financial Handbook

As we all know, one of the great things about the United States is that anyone who works hard, saves their money, and takes care of themselves is able to achieve the American Dream. But unfortunately, we also know that someone always wants a piece of the American Dream, and that someone is the taxman.

Everyone pays taxes, and almost all of us insist we're paying too much. "Why should someone who's worked hard and saved their money their whole life have to pay more than someone who's lazy?" a lot of us ask. In fact, I'm willing to bet that you agree. Do you think you're paying too much in taxes? I bet so; otherwise you wouldn't be reading this book.

Well, I have good news and bad news. The bad news is that you probably are paying too much in taxes. In fact, I'm often asked which political party would be better for the economy and taxes: Democrats or Republicans. I don't have an answer. The only thing we can be certain of is the nature of politicians.

If we break apart the word politics, you get the two Greek root words *poli* and *tic*. *Poli* means many, and *tic* means blood sucker, so no matter who gets into office, we can be certain they will always find a way to take our money.

Fortunately, the good news is that this book will help you learn how to stop paying so much in taxes.

Let's take a quick look at some of the other things we'll be discussing:

• Long-Term Care

Have you been solicited for LTC in the past six months? (If not, I want to know your secret!) Long Term Care is a growing area of concern for seniors, and we'll look at what your advisor may not know about LTC.

• Estates

As time goes on, caring and providing for our families becomes more and more important. But what happens to your family if someone is overlooked, or your advisor makes a mistake in your estate?

• Probate

Most of us know that there are court costs associated with probate, but have you and your advisor prepared for attorney costs? You'll also find out why banks and brokers profit from your probate.

• Taxes

We'll look at income taxes, Social Security taxes, and even estate taxes throughout the book. In fact, you may not realize it, but even the money and investments you leave behind for your family will be taxed. So we'll discuss how to minimize the taxes associated with your inheritance.

• Advisors

This is perhaps the most important topic of this book. If you follow the news, you know that there seems to be a constant stream of lawsuits filed against investment bankers, analysts, and stockbrokers, most of whom have to do with fraud perpetrated against investors like yourself. Are they all out to cheat you and steal your money? You'll learn how to protect yourself from unethical advisors who care more about lining their own pockets than about your investments.

When you get down to it, there's really three fundamental realities to investing: Reduce your taxes, beware of unethical stockbrokers and insurance agents, and achieve your investment goals with the least amount of risk. These have always been important, and now that the Internet boom of the 1990s is over, they've returned to the forefront of investing. This book will address all three things.

Like many senior investors, you've accumulated a lot of wealth over the last 40 years, and it's important to learn how to preserve it. The last thing anyone wants is for their life savings to disappear because of a bad decision, and the information I'm going to share with you will help avoid costly mistakes.

> *"There are two systems of taxation in our country: one for the informed and one for the uninformed."*
>
> —Justice Learned Hand, United States Appellate Court

When Justice Learned Hand, one of the greatest Appellate Court justices in our country's history, made the above statement, he meant that the uninformed people of the United States usually pay more in taxes than those who are informed. Not only is he right, but informed people who do not act on their knowledge also have no advantage over others who are uniformed. So if you want to improve your portfolio, reduce your taxes, and avoid unethical stockbrokers, it's not enough to simply read this book. In order for the advice in this book to be of any benefit, you'll need to act upon what you'll learn.

Learning From the U.S. Navy

Whenever Navy ships come into port, they always test the ship's anchor chains. If you've been in the U.S. Navy or taken a tour of one of their ships, you've probably noticed that the anchor is attached to the ship by a huge chain with links of steel that are well over five inches thick.

Why, then, are the chains tested each time the ships docks in port? Surely those chains never break, and no sailor who has been at sea for months wants to spend time testing each link of such a huge chain when they're about to go on leave.

Well, the Navy does this because they want to know if there is a problem with the chain before it breaks. It's called a stress test, and it's almost always a good idea in any situation – even investing.

My point is that you should always find out if something's wrong before problems arise. The same holds true for investing. If you hold technology stocks, when do you want to find out if they're worthless: now or in two years when the company goes bankrupt? If you have Long Term Care insurance, do you want to find out about potential problems with your coverage now or once you're in a nursing home? If you've mistakenly disinherited your grandchildren, would you like to know about it now, when it can be fixed, or let it go and hope that everything works out when you're gone?

Stress tests will make sure that everything in your portfolio and financial documents has been taken care of before it's too late, and you'll learn stress tests for several areas of your finances throughout this book.

CHAPTER 2

The Greatest Generation

As senior investors, there's no question that you've worked long and hard for everything you have. In fact, your generation built this country. You fought World War II, then came home to re-create the United States as the most powerful nation in the world. You built communities, businesses, and a strong government while also developing sciences and the arts. You put a man on the moon and provided women the opportunity to enter the workforce.

More importantly, your sacrifices and hard work changed the course of American history. And through it all, you never complained.

Yet today, as grandparents and retirees, how are you rewarded for your years of struggle and hard work? By paying high taxes? By supporting people who have just moved to this country, yet have never paid a single dollar in taxes? If you become sick and need to be hospitalized in a long- term care facility for an extended period of time, who pays for it? You do, of course. And just how long are you expected to pay for your stay? Until you're broke.

Compare that to many of our nation's policies on health care for the uninsured and immigrants in this country, and you're likely to become angry. For example, if a brand new immigrant moves to the United States, then becomes ill and needs hospitalization, do they pay for it? Of course not. Government programs pay for their medical needs, and taxpayers like you fund these programs.

This is not to say that immigrants should not receive medical assistance, or that we should turn these people away. In fact, one of the great things about your generation is that you've encouraged people across the world to come here, work hard, and reach the success you've had. You should not be treated so unfairly.

You've paid your dues to this country. You've given the United States your hard work and sweat for more than 40 years, but once you need help, the government does nothing until you're broke. It doesn't exactly seem fair, does it?

The Rules of the Game

When situations like this occur, we often believe that other people get special treatment; that we're missing out on something because we play by the rules. We may feel helpless, forced to stand by and watch while others cheat to get what they want.

In the real world, cheaters eventually get caught. We hear about people who falsify medical information in order to qualify for treatments or surgeries. Executives and firms on Wall Street get fined because they're caught cheating investors. People like Ken Lay at Enron and Dennis Kozlowski of Tyco are held personally accountable for using their companies as a personal piggy bank. But how are they punished? Are they required to return the billions they've stolen from middle-income America? Not hardly. They get a few years in a country club prison and get to keep the billions they stole.

So while cheaters do get caught, others seem to get ahead and get special treatment. Why? Because they know the rules of the game. Whether it's taxes, investing, or your finances, some people are able to take advantage of situations because they know the rules. On the other hand, you may be stuck watching people get ahead because there are rules you don't understand or don't even know about.

Have you ever played a game with someone where you didn't know all the rules, but the other person knew them inside and out? Who won? Most likely, they did – and not because they cheated. They just knew the rules better than you.

When it comes to taxes, investing, and your finances, there are a lot of rules out there you are not even aware of. This book is going to make sure you know and understand some of these rules. However, it is up to you to use them if you want to get ahead. Trust me, the rulebook can work in your favor if you use it to your advantage.

An Informed Consumer

This book is also going to discuss a wide variety of topics in several areas. While you have already been given an overview of these things, it's in no way comprehensive. Actually, any of the topics we're going to discuss could probably be a book by itself.

But remember that no book can determine what is important to you right now. IRAs, municipal bonds, estates, long-term care – your situation is unique to you and your family, so some topics are going to be more important to you than others. The important thing is that you make notes as you read these chapters, and ask your qualified senior advisor about these topics the next time you speak with him or her.

CHAPTER **3**

An Overview of the Financial Services Industry

B efore we discuss the nuts and bolts of senior financial planning, it's necessary to understand where senior investors fit into the financial planning community as a whole. After all, you can't accurately know what to expect from your advisor if you don't understand the business and how seniors are viewed by the financial services industry.

A Quick History of Financial Planning

The financial services industry may have been around for years, but the idea of financial planning is relatively new by comparison. And for our purposes, as well as your best interest, you need to think about financial services as financial planning. Although stockbrokers have been selling products since before J.P. Morgan made his first million, we're only concerned with what applies to you – and selling things to people simply for a commission is not in your best interest. So while Wall Street has a long and interesting history, most of it is not going to make a difference to your needs.

Financial planning, however, is a young industry. Unlike the traditional model of stockbrokers, who sell products to anyone who would buy them for a commission, financial planning requires that an advisor look at the whole picture of their client's financial situation and help them solve any of a variety of issues they may face. (If you remember my personal history from the Introduction, you'll see how I evolved from a traditional stockbroker to a financial planner in my own career.)

The concept of financial planning really began in the 1970's with two mutual fund companies, Vanguard and Fidelity, as well as American Express. These firms began to see the value in not just selling investments, but helping clients select the right investment for their needs. As this evolved, financial planning grew to include complementary services and a wider variety of products in order to meet the growing needs of clients. No longer was it good enough to simply sell a product to a client. Advisors were now interested in their clients' financial goals, such as their children's college and retirement, as well as capital gains, tax implications, and other issues that were impacting their investments.

As the years went on, the concept of financial planning became more accepted by the general public, and as investors realized the value of this service, they grew to demand more from their stockbroker than a list of products and a sales pitch. The increased demand caused major Wall Street investment banks to begin offering their own version of financial planning as well. Soon companies like Merrill Lynch and Piper Jaffray (which is now part of UBS) had jumped on the bandwagon, touting financial plans as the new evolution in financial services in order to remain competitive and keep clients.

Today, financial planning has become an integral part of the financial services industry. No matter where you go, be it a wirehouse, a regional firm, or an independent advisor, financial planning is now an expected part of an advisor's job. Yet, as we'll discuss in a later chapter, not all financial planners are the same.

Senior Financial Planning

We all need different things at different times in our lives, and this applies to our finances as well. So it should come as no surprise that seniors need a different kind of financial planning than other investors.

Think about it. Do you have the same debt problems that your children have? Probably not. You may owe a few thousand on a car loan or a hospital bill, but your children are still paying off college, as well as thousands of dollars in credit card debt, if they're like most baby boomers.

Do you have the same investment problems that your children have? Probably not. You need to make sure you have enough for things like long-term care and are concerned with holding onto the money you have so you can enjoy your retirement. Your children, on the other hand, are desperately trying to save enough so they can afford to retire, not to mention saving for their own children's college education.

Do you have the same health problems that your children have? Absolutely not. You may have existing conditions that require hundreds or thousands of dollars of medications each year, as well as expensive medical treatments and specialists. Seniors realize that maintaining the human body is not cheap. Baby boomers like your children are just now beginning to have occasional health problems, as their eyes start to deteriorate, the occasional back pain becomes more common, and chronic conditions such as high cholesterol start to raise their ugly heads.

Actually, your finances have nothing in common with your children's. So why compare your investments and financial situation to your children and others who are at different stages in their lives and need different things from their money? The fact is, you shouldn't.

Unlike most financial plans that focus on making more money, senior planning makes sure you keep what you have and helps you avoid paying unnecessary taxes. An advisor who specializes in senior planning should be willing to review your taxes, your beneficiaries and titling, your catastrophic protection, and your legal affairs, all on an annual basis. How many run-of-the-mill advisors do that?

Yet seniors are told they should continue to think and invest like everyone else.

When I ask seniors how they are doing financially, most people say "Great! I made 'this much' last year," or "Terrible! I lost 'this much' last year." But does it really matter how much money you made last year? Not as much as most people think.

> At this stage in your life, you're probably not as interested in making money as you are in keeping it.

At this stage in your life, you're probably not as interested in making money as you are in keeping it. You're interested in planning your affairs. You realize that you don't have 20 or 30 years to make money, so you want to make the most of what you have. That's the essence of senior planning.

Don't believe me? Well, let's say that you had a huge rate of return last year. Would you go buy a yacht? How about a vacation home? Would it change your lifestyle at all? On the other hand, what if you ended up giving two-thirds of that huge return back to Uncle Sam in taxes? Or it's unexpectedly eaten up by bills for long-term care. Or that your affairs are so jumbled up and such a mess that once you die, your spouse doesn't understand anything and makes some bad decisions?

These are all very real examples of the financial problems seniors face every day. And if you want to avoid these kinds of issues, you need to stop planning your finances as if you were a newlywed and start planning your finances to reflect the concerns you have. Trust me, you'll thank me later.

And because of your unique situation, you and every other senior investor in the country should have an advisor who understands your unique situation and can cater to your investment needs. Just as some financial advisors cater to the ultra-wealthy and specialize in helping multi-millionaires manage their money, there are advisors who are trained to specifically handle the needs of seniors like yourself. And if the AARP can make Capitol Hill cater to the needs of seniors, shouldn't advisors do the same?

The Good and The Bad

But as with everything, there are some great things about the current world of financial planning and some problems you need to be mindful of.

The good news is that most Certified Financial Planners, or CFP®s, and Certified Senior Advisors, are likely to be independent advisors, which means there will be less conflict of interest and a wider range of options available to you. If you recall my own personal experience, I realized how difficult it is to do what's best for a client when you're only able to offer your firm's products and services.

Independent advisors, on the other hand, have the freedom to offer products and services they truly believe in, without any pressure from an employing firm. So one of the good developments in the financial planning arena is that many financial planners have left wirehouses and firms to become independent. Most advisors do this because they want to do what's right for their clients. And fortunately, this trend continues today.

The bad news, however, is that the core beliefs behind financial planning are deteriorating as more and more brokers jump on the financial planning bandwagon. You've already heard my opinions about the CFP Board and how what used to be a great organization has caused controversy among planners such as myself.

Many professionals believe that the CFP Board has lost its moral compass and that by allowing wirehouses to freely give out the CFP® designation, the standards behind the certification are rapidly dropping. So while such designations as these are intended to represent an advisor's knowledge and ethics, you should rely on your own intuition as to whether or not your advisor has your best interests at heart.

Now that you've got a better understanding of what financial planning is all about, let's take a look at Wall Street and why investors such as yourself have been treated so badly.

How Did This Happen?

Wall Street has never been easy to understand, but in recent years the road for investors has gotten even rockier. It's hard enough to decide where to put your money when the market's doing well, but these days it's a whole different ballgame. Company earnings announcements are more complicated than the IRS tax code. The difference between comparable mutual funds is like splitting hairs. As if that's not enough, investors now have to contend with a landslide of recent corporate scandals. Not surprisingly, just planning for your retirement in the 21st Century is akin to walking through a minefield.

Corporate greed made headlines back in the 1980's thanks to Michael Milken, junk bonds, and the movie *Wall Street*. The general public's skepticism towards investing was at an all-time high, and watching actor Michael Douglas portray a greedy investment tycoon confirmed our opinions. When his character, Gordon Gekko, told a roomful of stockbrokers that "*Greed is good,*" our distrust of the financial services industry was solidified.

But once the 80's ended, the market took a turn for the worse. Everyone, including the Gordon Gekkos of the world, was losing money, and investors had more important things to worry about than whether or not their stockbroker was a sleazy salesman cheating them out of better returns. Eventually, the frustration of the early 1990's gave way to the dot-com boom. On the eve of a new millennium, we watched our economy grow faster than it ever had, transformed by technology and a new form of communication called the Internet. No longer was the future about flying cars and trips to outer space. The future had arrived, and it was about connectivity, speed, and the ability to see or do anything at the click of a button.

Wall Street took notice by investing in the phenomenon heavily and rapidly. Twenty-somethings who were running websites out of their parent's basements were given millions of dollars based on nothing more than a vague plan and a few computers. And for a while, it worked. Everyone owned Internet and technology stocks, and we considered taking our money out of tried-and-true successes like the S&P 500 because some new company with a name we couldn't spell was seeing quarterly double-digit earnings.

> Anything that looks too good to be true probably is.

But as we all know: anything that looks too good to be true, probably is. And, of course, this was the case with the dot-com boom of the late 90's. Common sense finally came back to Wall Street, and once investors realized that most of these Internet companies were never going to be profitable, we cut our losses and regained our wits.

Unfortunately, it wasn't just investors who were swayed by the excitement of this period. Companies and financial firms alike expected to see huge profits and growth, and many of them would do anything to get them. So although many of us lost our shirts when the bubble burst, some corporations weren't willing to admit they'd done the same. Rather than admit their mistakes, they began a dangerous charade – one where the company pretended to be profitable while executives stole money and left investors, such as yourself, footing the bill.

Enron: A Tale of Lies and Cover-ups

At the beginning of 1991, Enron was an example of corporate success and a stock sought after by investors. The company's profits continued to rise quarter after quarter, and its executives lived like kings.

But by December of that year, everything had changed. Enron had declared bankruptcy, creating the biggest corporate collapse in American history. As a result, many investors and employees were left broke, a vice chairman committed suicide and Arthur Andersen, the energy giant's accounting firm, was destroyed for looking the other way while executives used corporate expense accounts for everything from personal cell phones to trips to adult clubs.

Enron first became successful because it took advantage of utility deregulation in the late 80's. At the time, users were allowed to buy gas or electricity from any number of producers, and the company made a lot of its money by selling contracts to deliver natural gas and other forms of energy in the future. But in August 2001, chief executive officer Jeffrey Skilling abruptly left the company, leaving investors and analysts worried. Soon the company's stock price began to drop, even though its chairman, Kenneth Lay insisted things were fine.

That October, the company set aside $35 million to reflect losses from two partnerships. As investors, regulators, and the general public began to ask questions, it was discovered that the partnerships had been set up in 1999 to conceal the corporation's overwhelming debt. Once the truth came to light, Enron was forced to restate and "correct" its numbers, which resulted in a $1.2 billion loss in equity. Shareholders of Enron saw their investments fall through the floor, and the company's stock spiraled downward.

Investigators discovered that not only were Enron executives using corporate funds for personal purchases and expenses, but that they also had been covering their tracks for years. Arthur Andersen, the company's auditor, also was raked over the coals for destroying documents and taking part in the charade.

As a result of this mess, Arthur Andersen was found guilty of obstructing justice and has been closed down in the United States. Enron executives such as Kenneth Lay are under investigation and indictment for conspiracy and fraud charges, and many employees of the corporation watched their retirement funds disappear.

Sadly, while Enron has been the most significant example of corporate greed in recent years, it's far from an isolated incident. Other companies such as Global Crossing and World Com declared bankruptcy around the same time, and even Wall Street firms such as JP Morgan Chase and Citigroup were tarnished by their involvement in the scandal. In 2003, the two investment banks agreed to pay a combined $255 million to settle charges that they helped Enron commit fraud.

But What About Brokerage Firms and Mutual Funds?

Of course, we can look at Enron and tell ourselves, "That's just one company. At least my mutual funds are diverse enough to help soften the damage any one company might make to my portfolio." Even though that makes sense, it's a dangerous assumption. But by not putting all our eggs in one basket, we lull ourselves into a false sense of security, thinking that we'll be immune from any future scandals. Sadly, it's just not true.

It was hard enough when investors realized that some corporations have acted unethically and lied to investors to make money. But just when it seemed corporate accountability was starting to improve, the mutual fund industry was shaken by a similar scandal in late 2003.

In September of that year, New York Attorney General Eliot Spitzer settled with hedge fund company Canary Capital on charges regarding mutual fund trading abuses. During the investigation and settlement, four additional fund companies, Janus Capital, Strong Financial, Bank of America, and Bank One, were also implicated.

Before long, things began to steamroll as Spitzer and the Securities and Exchange Commission (SEC) found that these companies weren't the only ones breaking the rules. By November, over 20 companies were involved in the scandal, including such Wall Street heavyweights as Bear Stearns, Merrill Lynch, Smith Barney, UBS, Wachovia, and Morgan Stanley. In fact, that same month, Morgan Stanley agreed to pay $50 million to settle charges that the brokerage firm did not tell investors that it was receiving compensation for selling certain mutual funds.

Mutual Fund Myths

- **Funds are long-term investments.**

  424 funds disappeared in 2002, and 24% of funds that existed in 1986 are now gone.

- **Managers have the discipline to hold long-term.**

  Turnover rates have gone from 15-20% in 1950 to over 110% in 2002.

- **Fund costs are declining as they grow in size.**

  On average, fund costs have doubled.

This kind of revenue sharing, which happens when mutual fund companies pay kickbacks to brokerages for encouraging investors to buy their funds, was happening all over the place. Following Spitzer's lead, the SEC announced that the act was "common practice" after conducting their own investigation of the fund industry. According to their study, about half of the brokerages they targeted paid their stockbrokers extra money when they sold shares of these particular funds.

Essentially, these companies were making trades that caused individual investors such as yourself to lose money. These companies were doing something called "late trading." This is when investors illegally buy or sell shares after the market's close, but still get the closing price. Mutual funds are priced once a day, at the close of the market, and orders placed after that time are supposed to use the next day's closing price.

This may not sound like a big deal, but if important news is announced after the market closes, these late traders were almost guaranteed a profit, or at least avoided a loss.

Why is this such a big deal? Well, besides the fact that it was illegal, these companies were taking other people's profits. For example, let's say a mutual fund with $500 million grows an additional $10 million during a day of trading. Now, let's say that a hedge fund invested an additional $50 million in late trading, and that they got that day's price. Instead of the $10 million in profit being spread among the original $500 million, it's now spread among $550 million – which means that investors like you get a smaller piece of profit, while a company that hadn't even invested in the fund makes a huge return.

Not surprisingly, the fallout from all this scheming was pretty significant. Lawrence Lasser, the CEO of Putnam Investments, lost his job, as did Richard Strong, CEO of Strong Financial. In fact, the scandal even impacted the SEC. During the investigation, the head of the SEC's Boston office resigned because he knew about some of these companies' activities, but looked the other way.

What Should I Do?

Senior investors regularly ask me if they should be concerned about their mutual funds. The truth is both yes and no. Although mutual funds have grown to a seven trillion dollar business, most of the fund companies involved were smaller in size.

However, even the gold standards of the mutual fund industry, including Fidelity, Vanguard, and American Funds, have been found to be involved in these shady practices, so few mutual fund investors remained unscathed.

But looking at the brokerage side of the scandal, just about every major wirehouse in the country was involved in some way, so even though your broker may be an upstanding businessperson, he or she can't speak for his or her whole firm.

The bottom line is that there's no need to completely avoid mutual funds (or individual stocks) because of what's happened. But what you should do is learn from these scandals and make sure that nothing you own – stocks or funds – are involved in any shady business. How can you be sure? You can start by having a financial advisor whom you trust to review your investments for these issues. These scandals impact companies and funds that have high amounts of growth and a lot of investor turnover.

Will Things Change?

While these scandals have certainly rocked Wall Street, that doesn't mean the stock market's nothing but gamblers and cheaters. There are still great, ethical companies that make money for their shareholders and plenty of funds that haven't been involved in any wrong doing.

And when you think about it, such scandals are mere bumps in the road – if you're investing for the long haul. However, as we've said in previous chapters, senior investors shouldn't be in the accumulation phase of their investing lives, and these kind of events usually cause problems for people who are out to make a quick buck. So if you're on track to retain your assets and enjoy the rest of your life, odds are you'll be watching from the sidelines the next time something like this happens.

> But sadly, these kinds of scandals aren't going to stop. After all, Wall Street has always attracted more than its fair share of crooks...

But sadly, these kinds of scandals aren't going to stop. After all, Wall Street has always attracted more than its fair share of crooks, and that's not going to change. The good news is that these kinds of isolated scandals seldom bring the market to a halt, either. Think about it. Neither Enron nor the mutual fund scandal of 2003 caused the kind of stock crash we saw after the dot-com boom of the 90's. It's unlikely that one area of investing is going to cause everything to drop, no matter what's being done.

So while no one can predict the future, you can make sure your chances of being involved in a future scandal are minimized. The best way to do that is to follow the advice in the next chapter and find an advisor who has your best interests in mind. You'll learn how to pick a good advisor, what to look for, and things to keep in mind as you evaluate your current financial professional.

CHAPTER 4

Use an Advisor or Do-it-yourself?

Like many senior investors, you're probably using some sort of financial advisor. You may be working with a broker, an insurance agent, a mutual fund salesperson, a CD or savings account salesperson, or an accountant. And like many financial consultants, they may call themselves an advisor. But are they?

The Merriam-Webster dictionary defines an advisor as someone who provides counsel, as well as warnings, recommendations, and concerns. It also defines an advisor as someone who provides information. In other words, a true advisor gives you his or her informed and knowledgeable opinion, along with warnings about risks and consequences.

In the world of financial advice, an advisor is someone who gives guidance based on both existing and predicted conditions. An advisor should be your advisor and confidante. For example, taxes are an existing and ongoing condition that your advisor should be able to provide advice on. Also, things like the possibility of needing long- term care are predicted conditions, and your advisor should be able to provide information about these kinds of things, as well as their benefits and potential risks.

Do I Need a New Advisor?

One of the most important things you can do is ask yourself the following: "Am I using an advisor, or is he or she a salesperson?"

> **Is your current advisor giving you advice and options about the topics that are important to you?**

If you're not sure, look at your concerns and financial plans for the future. Is your current advisor giving you advice and options about the topics that are important to you? If you ask him or her about long-term care, is he or she able to explain the pros and cons of various plans, as well as the impact this coverage will have on your portfolio and budget?

For example, if you've already asked your advisor about estate planning, but still remain confused or uncertain as to how a trust works, they're clearly not giving you satisfactory information or making you aware of all your options. In many of these situations, your advisor may be nothing more than a salesperson who is able to explain his or her products.

Also, if you hear about techniques that could put you in a better position, but your financial professional has never told you about them, there are two possible explanations. Either your advisor doesn't know about them, or he or she simply doesn't care. Of course, neither answer is one you want to hear.

There are certain things you should expect from your advisor, and here's a general list to help you think about your current financial advisor.

- ## Integrity

It's essential that you trust your advisor. An advisor with integrity takes his or her responsibilities and your expectations seriously and knows that principles are more important than his or her own personal gain.

- ## Connectivity

Your advisor should be part of a network or group whose sole mission is to put seniors' goals and needs first by pooling experience, expertise, and knowledge, as well as sharing it for the better good. Good examples of this are the National Council on Aging and the National Senior Resource Center.

- ## Objectivity

Every recommendation your advisor makes should be based solely on what's best for you, and he or she should not suggest products or services that don't meet your needs or financial goals. Good advisors use their experience and knowledge to carefully consider your situation, then provide advice based on what will best meet your goals.

- ## Competency

Your advisor should be knowledgeable about the products or services he or she recommends and offers. More importantly, your advisor should never offer advice about products or services he or she isn't qualified and licensed to provide. Advisors who do so are breaking the law.

- ## Privacy

You give your advisor personal information about your financial status, as well as other personal information. In return, your advisor should not share this information with anyone else, unless you give him or her permission to do so when conducting business on your behalf. The only exception to this is if your advisor is ordered by a court of law to provide this information.

Whether or not you need a new advisor is a question you'll have to answer yourself, but trust your instincts. As a paid professional, your advisor should be able to completely explain and address every aspect of your financial concerns. If not, you may need to consider looking for someone else.

What Consumer Reports Found

In January 1998, *Consumer Reports* ran a report in their magazine about a secret shopper who went to several financial advisors. Now, if you're not familiar with *Consumer Reports*, a secret shopper is someone who pretends to be a normal shopper, but records everything that goes on. After visiting the businesses, the shopper then writes a report about their findings and compares how the companies treat consumers.

In this report, the secret shopper went to five advisors; one with American Express, one with Merrill Lynch, one with Prudential Securities, and two independent advisors. The shopper found that two of those five advisors were superior to the others. Which advisors do you think came out on top?

Yep, it was the independent advisors. But why do you think this was the case?

The shopper went on to explain that only the two independent advisors addressed all of his goals. He also said that while all the finished plans looked slick and professional, the other advisors recommended products that came from their own company.

It's not surprising. Talk to a friend who invests with Merrill Lynch, and they're likely to own Merrill Lynch mutual funds. Ask someone who invests with American Express the same question, and they will probably say they have American Express products in their portfolio. Advisors do this because it's good for business, plain and simple. Of course, it's good for their business, but that doesn't necessarily mean it's good for yours.

Let's say you've decided to buy your grandson a car for his birthday. You've also decided that it needs to be safe and reliable and get good gas mileage. So you go to your local Nissan dealership and tell the salesperson that you want a reliable, economical car that gets good gas mileage.

"Oh, sure," he tells you, "You should test drive a Toyota Tercel. The dealership is just down the street on the left."

Is that what the salesperson would say to you? Not likely. No Nissan salesperson would recommend a Toyota, or a Honda, or any other type of car because it would be bad for business. How would a car salesperson make any money if he or she recommended cars that weren't on his or her lot, even if another brand was better for you?

Now apply that logic to advisors. Why do you think advisors with a big firm or wirehouse recommend that you buy their fund? Is it possible that out of 17,000 mutual funds, theirs just happens to be the best? It's possible, but the odds certainly aren't in their favor. Like the car salesperson, advisors do this so they and their firms can make more money, and the term for these biased recommendations is a "preferred list."

Have you ever tried to move proprietary funds, such as a Merill Lynch mutual fund or American Express annuity, from one firm to another? It's not possible. It doesn't matter what firms you're talking about, you can't say, "Well, I'd like to take $10,000 in proprietary funds out of my portfolio and move it over to my account at this other firm." You can't even get firms to move your funds to accounts you might have with independent advisors. The bottom line is that firms that have you invested in their funds will not let you move them out of their firm.

Simply put, firms have you handcuffed to their products and services. And if you do move, you're hit with all kinds of charges and fees like a slap on the wrist. If you own B shares, there's surrender charges and possible taxes. So if you have a proprietary mutual fund, you have to ask yourself, "Did my advisor suggest this because it was the best thing for me, or did he or she do it to make money for him or herself and prevent me from leaving the firm?" And that's a question only you can answer.

Financial Consumer Scorecard

It is how you invest, not what you invest in, that will determine your ultimate success.

How many investment companies, advisors and planners realize protecting your money means protecting your future? How many actually care if you achieve your goals or end up struggling to make ends meet? How many fully appreciate the fundamental importance of protecting your money?

This comparison scorecard is designed for practical people who are interested in evaluating and filtering information to ensure the advice they receive is in their best interest.

This scorecard provides a comparison between what we know is possible and the unfortunate reality many practical investors face. By assessing your current situation we hope this document helps you protect your money and your future.

	What's Truly Possible	The Unfortunate Reality
Your Empowerment and Education	Consumer Advocacy - Advice and help that begins with taking your goals into account. Someone who will tell you the truth about the investment industry. Access to the fundamental concepts and principles of successful investing.	Advice based on an agenda to sell products and services. Advice based on what is best for the investment advisor. Product- or service- specific advice only. Limited sharing to support an agenda other than their own.
Diligent Discovery	First, your advisors discover if they can actually help you in the long term.	"Our products and services are right for everyone."
Rigorous Analysis	A complete analysis of what you have is complete before any possible solutions are suggested.	There is little or no analysis of your present financial situation.
Simple and Easy to Follow Plan	The foundation for a plan is created by analysis and an honest appraisal of your strengths and weaknesses.	There is either no plan at all or they provide a pre-formatted "cookie cutter" plan that is obsolete as soon as it is put on the table."This is the way it is always done," is used to justify a pace beyond your comfort zone.
Guaranteed Portfolio	Only solutions with guarantees attached are offered. The quest for performance is less important than ensuring you do not lose what you already have.	Your hard-earned assets are vulnerable. Chasing returns often lead to losing sight of protecting existing assets.
Living Plan	Your investments are continuosly monitored to ensure you live to the highest means possible without fear of running out of money.	Your expectations are manipulated.

Take the Retirement $tress Test

(The Three Little Pigs Test)

Check the following statements that apply to you to determine how your financial foundation would survive the Big Bad Wolf.

__ I understand how the taxation system and the brokerage and banking industries pertain to me and how I can use these systems to my full advantage.

__ I know that I am paying the least amount of tax legally possible.

__ I feel that every year all available techniques to benefit my situation are fully explained.

__ I spend as much as I want without worry of running out of money.

__ I have clear, written goals and plans to achieve them.

__ I have reviewed all the hybrid investment techniques developed in the last 5 years.

__ I know how much, within $100, I pay in tax as a result of my investments.

— I understand how the tax law changes of July 2001 (EGTRRA) affect my family. I have utilized it to pass on a significantly higher percentage of my assets to my heirs.

— I have reviewed all long-term care options (LTC, Insurance, Asset-Backed Protection, Kennedy-Kassenbaum Plan) and am comfortable with my selection.

— I'm in control of my financial fate, NOT the other way around. I control my finances, my finances do not control or limit me.

🐺 Score

1-4 House made of **straw**
5-8 House made of **sticks**
9-10 House made of **bricks**

Getting back to *Consumer Reports*, the shopper ended the report by saying "In hindsight, I think I would have been better off building my relationship with planners more gradually by having them focus on specific issues such as retirement planning."

What the shopper found out is that if you have college funding issues, go to a college funding specialist. If you're a business owner and you have 401(k) issues, go to a 401(k) specialist. So if you're retired and have estate planning and long-term care issues, go to a retirement specialist who understands the needs of senior investors, namely a Certified Senior Advisor or an affiliate of the National Senior Resource Center.

Fifty years ago, there was only one kind of doctor – the kind you went to when you were sick. But today, there's specialists in every type of field you could imagine. Doctors specialize in allergies, skin problems, heart problems, and there's podiatrists, gynecologists, oncologists, even specialized surgeons. So if you have a heart problem, would you go see a doctor who specializes in the human foot? Of course not. You'd go to a heart specialist. So why let an advisor who specializes in college planning (or worse yet, doesn't have a specialty) handle your financial concerns?

What Should You Delegate?

Of course, there are bound to be some things you can do on your own, and you may find that you're capable of handling certain aspects of your finances by yourself without professional help. If so, that's great.

For example, some people like to take care of their own investments. They enjoy keeping up with their returns, learning about new products they might want to invest in, researching companies, and keeping tabs on Wall Street in general. If you're one of those people, you may want to handle your portfolio yourself rather than hand it over to an advisor.

Other people like to keep track of their expenses and spending. These people love having computer programs that balance their checkbooks, remind them of bills that are due, and help them calculate their taxes. If you're one of those people, you may enjoy handling these things yourself rather than hiring an accountant.

The point is that if you love doing something, then by all means, continue to do it. But if you hate researching stocks and reading the *Wall Street Journal*, then delegate your portfolio to a capable advisor. Likewise, if you hate dealing with numbers, and the thought of doing your own taxes makes you cringe, then delegate those duties to an accountant.

> If you decide to do something like your taxes or investments yourself, make sure you're just as knowledgeable and capable as a professional.

But there is a catch to doing these things yourself. If you decide to do something like your taxes or your investments yourself, make sure you are just as knowledgeable and capable as a professional. Because if you can't do something as well and as conveniently as a professional can, it'll be more trouble than it's worth.

For example, when I was in my 20's, I used to change the oil in my car myself and would even give my car tune-ups. I don't do either of those things anymore. Could I if I wanted to? Of course, but it's more convenient for me to pay someone else to maintain my car than to spend a Saturday afternoon doing it myself.

Also, no matter how much you enjoy doing tasks like these, you'll need to not only be competent in your abilities, but commit to staying on top of them. Because when you decide to do something like select your own stocks, file your own taxes, or write your own will, you've chosen not to use a professional – and that means you are the professional.

To demonstrate just how important this is, consider your annual tax return. You may be able to fill out a 1040 yourself, but a good accountant keeps up on the new tax laws and can give advice as to how to best reduce taxes, take advantage of tax credits, and avoid things like the alternative minimum tax and an audit. If you're going to take care of your taxes yourself, you should understand all these things as well as a professional does. If not, you're better off using an accountant. It may cost more, but you're also getting a lot more for your money.

Likewise, you may be able to buy software that will allow you to draft your own will and handle basic legal matters, but how will you know if something's incorrect or the laws change? Do you want to run the risk of disinheriting members of your family because a computer program gave you incorrect information or didn't notify you of a law change? Of course not. So unless you're an attorney yourself, you'd be wise to spend money on a good lawyer. Because even if you're sure you can do it yourself, there's a high risk to doing so.

The most popular thing people handle on their own is their investments, and that's great. After all, it's your money – you should be keeping tabs on it. During the Internet boom of the 1990's, the mainstream media began referring to investing as the Great American Hobby. And it's no surprise really. Thanks to advances in technology anyone with a few shares of stock can watch live market activity on CNBC, research stocks online with companies like Morningstar, and even buy and sell their own stocks over the internet. And people who do this on a regular basis are usually very capable of taking care of their own investments. But if you're one of those people, you need to realize that it'll become a big part of your life. Once you commit to handling all your investments on your own, you have to have a constant eye on the market every single day. In today's Wall Street, you can't keep up with your stocks one day and forget about them the next.

So no matter what duties you decide to take on yourself, remember that it's not a hobby. Things like gardening, woodwork, and golf are hobbies. Guarding and securing everything you've earned from 40 years of hard work is not. It's a full-time job that you shouldn't take lightly.

The bottom line is that you need to spend at least three or four hours a day on any task that you decide to handle yourself. So if you enjoy taxes or investing that much, good for you. You'll probably give yourself more attention than a professional would. But if that kind of commitment doesn't sound like fun, don't feel bad. A lot of people are very capable of doing these kinds of tasks, but decided there are better ways to spend their time. Either way, you're going to benefit.

Resources for You to Do It Yourself

Of course, if you decide to take on any of these services yourself, you're going to need resources to help you. While I'm not an expert on taxes or law, here are some things to assist those of you who plan on handling your own investments.

As we've already mentioned, the Internet is your best tool when it comes to investments. There is a multitude of resources out there for do-it-yourself investors, such as Value Line (*http://. www.valueline.com*), Morningstar (*http://www.morningstar.com*), and Motley Fool (*http://www.fool.com*). There are also websites that specialize in helping investors with various kinds of investments, as well as subscription websites that provide third-party analysis of stocks and funds. Even the web portal Yahoo! has a great financial resource (*http://finance.yahoo.com*). As you can imagine, this is by no means a comprehensive list of web resources, but it should provide you with a good starting point to begin working in this area.

There are also organizations you can join for support and help. One of the most popular is the American Association of Individual Investors, or the AAII (*http://www.aaii.com*). There's also the National Association of Investors Corporation, or the NAIC (*http://www.better-investing.org*). Both provide a wealth of information for individual investors of all kinds, as well as a way to network and learn from others. Everyone who handles their own investments should join one such group.

Finally, there are plenty of print resources. You may already be familiar with the *Wall Street Journal*, but there's also *Investor's Business Daily,* as well as the *Financial Times.* And, as you well know, there's an abundance of magazines and books for individual investors – far more than this book could accurately address.

There is one important piece of advice for anyone handling their own investments. As you're looking for resources that will help you become a better and more knowledgeable investor, make sure you scrutinize everything you read. Not all editorial content is the same, and just because someone wrote it doesn't mean it's true.

> **Not all editorial content is the same, and just because someone wrote it doesn't mean it's true.**

So instead of looking for hot stock tips and the "next big thing," focus on information from multiple sources and make up your own mind. You should have at least five sources that you use on a regular basis to ensure that you're getting balanced information, and look for facts and figures, rather than someone telling you what to do. As with anything in life, anyone who tells you what to do has their own agenda and doesn't have your best interests at heart.

Those of you who want to do your own taxes should strongly consider J.K. Lasser's books (*http://www.jklasser.com*). Not only do his books help with filing taxes, but they are full of ideas and suggestions to reduce taxes as well. When it comes to computer software, Turbo Tax is an excellent program. In fact, if you truly want to understand as much as you can about taxes, take the tax classes offered by H&R Block on an annual basis. Information is available on their website (*http://www.hrblock.com*), and you'll learn most of the same things as their professional tax preparers. However, be sure to take refresher classes every year, in order to stay on top of the myriad tax law changes that continuously occur. It's an annual expense that could not only save you money in the long run, but may also give you the opportunity to work as a seasonal tax preparer.

When it comes to online resources, be careful. As with investments, don't assume that everything you read is correct. After all, if there's one organization that you don't want to cross, it's the IRS. Basically, you should make sure that any tax reduction strategy you use has been tried and true for many years. Unlike investing, taxes are one aspect of your life where you don't want to be ahead of the pack.

Lastly, there's the prospect of handling your own legal affairs, which is very risky. Unless you're an attorney, the risk of making a mistake or overlooking something is extremely great. In fact, handing your own legal affairs is almost like performing surgery on yourself. Doctors have their own doctors, and even lawyers have their own personal attorneys, so why should a novice such as yourself be any different?

There are lots of websites, books, and software out there that insist they can help you with things like wills and powers of attorney. Yet the problem is that every situation is different. So while they may provide a basic template for common, ordinary legal forms, the slightest difference from the norm makes them useless. And do you consider your financial situation to be common and ordinary? Probably not.

What Are You Trying to Accomplish?

So by now you're probably wondering, "Should I even use an advisor, or should I just do it myself?" Well, there's no easy answer, and the truth is that it depends on what you're trying to accomplish.

Unfortunately, no one can answer that question for you. But before you decide to go it alone, spend some time and assess your current situation. In other words, you have to step back and take a long, hard look at the big picture. For example, you need to find out your annual income. Do you expect it to go up or down in the future? How will your financial situation change if your spouse were to die? How will your financial situation change for your spouse if you were to die?

You also need to consider possible events that may impact your life. Is long-term care a possibility for you or your spouse? Is your home paid for? What would happen if you needed to move? What would happen if your children or grandchildren ever need a significant sum of money?

Cash flow is another area that you need to review. What are your expenses likely to be in the future? What kinds of things might change or interrupt your cash flow?

You also need to determine how long you and your spouse are likely to live. Is there a chance you'll run out of money? How much can you afford to spend annually? How much money do you need each month to maintain your current standard of living?

The last thing you'll need to consider is your legal and financial paperwork, because having the right things in place won't do much good if you forget a few key pieces of documentation. Does all your legal and financial paperwork list the correct beneficiaries? If you became incapacitated, will your spouse be able to handle your investments? What would happen to your investments if both you and your spouse were to die? Are you sure your investments will go to your children, or will Uncle Sam and the taxman get their hands on the American Dream you've built for yourself? Will your investments and years of hard work be lost to probate costs or attorney fees?

As you can see, there are a lot of questions you need to ask yourself, and you'll need to have thorough and complete answers to them. A guess or an estimate won't cut it. And as you might expect, it takes time to answer these questions thoroughly, not to mention the ongoing time commitment needed to stay on top of current information and changes in these areas. For example, are you willing to spend 10 or 15 hours a week doing the necessary research on tax law benefiting trusts, investments, and planning?

So sit down and ask yourself these questions, along with any others you think are important to you and your family's financial health. Once you do that you'll truly know where you stand. And that, in turn, will allow you to decide what you're trying to accomplish.

Maybe you're planning on leaving as much of your assets as possible to your children and grandchildren. Maybe you want to have a lifestyle of luxury and travel as a reward for all your years of hard work. Or maybe you simply want to live comfortably without ever worrying that you'll run out of money. No matter what the answer, you now have your financial goal.

Once you've answered these questions, you'll have a created a roadmap that will guide you throughout the rest of financial life.

How to Choose Advisors for Delegated Tasks

We've already discussed some traits that you should expect from a financial advisor and how to tell if you need a new one. But what should you do if it's time to move on and find a financial professional who cares more about your needs than lining their own pockets?

The most important thing you can do is look for someone who specializes in your needs and goals. Having already done the legwork of evaluating your current financial situation, you already know what you need to accomplish, so it's time to find someone who can fulfill those goals.

Yet finding a true specialist is easier said than done. For example, if you're looking to minimize your taxes on your investments, just about every advisor you speak to will insist that they can help you. And while they may have a product or two up their sleeve that they insist is tax-free, you'll have to do some legwork to evaluate them on your own. But don't worry; we'll get to that in a minute.

This applies to any financial professional you hire, be it an accountant, attorney, or insurance agent. For example, if you're looking for someone to do your taxes, make sure that the person you hire does taxes for a lot of people just like you – in other words, is familiar with retired individuals who hold significant investments. Likewise, business owners should find an accountant who specializes in taxes for small businesses. And if you have one professional who truly specializes in your needs, ask him or her for a referral. Odds are your accountant may know an insurance agent who specializes in long-term health care, or your financial advisor may know an attorney who regularly handles wills and estates for retired individuals.

When it comes to taxes, many people wonder if they need a Certified Public Accountant or if a tax preparer is enough. The truth is that a CPA is seldom necessary, unless you have a complicated situation. For example, if you've sold a significant amount of property or investments and are concerned about capital gains, an accountant might be worth the additional fee. But for the majority of us, tax preparers are fine for our needs.

Even individuals who file their own taxes should see a tax professional every few years. Anyone who does this should have an accountant review their tax forms once every three years, regardless of their situation. This will likely cost less than paying to have them done, and by getting them reviewed, you'll not only have made sure that everything's correct, but you may learn about a new law or tax change that affects you.

> Even individuals who file their own taxes should see a tax professional every few years.

When it comes to selecting a property casualty insurance agent, you should be diligent in interviewing potential agents. Ask them how they intend to make sure you're paying the least amount in fees every year, as well as how they plan to make sure you're always fully covered. Good agents have systems in place to keep up-to-date on their clients' needs.

You should use an independent agent, because like an independent advisor, they are able to shop around with several companies for the best deal possible. You can certainly interview proprietary agents, but you'll need to be skeptical. That's because a proprietary agent who works for one particular company only sells that company's products. And of course, if they can only sell one kind of policy, they're obviously going to insist that theirs is the best. That doesn't mean you shouldn't buy insurance from a proprietary agent, but it does mean that before you do, you had better be certain it's the best policy for you.

And thanks to the Internet, you can now even save money by cutting out the middleman. Companies like Geico (*http://www. geico.com*) and USAA (*http://www.usaa.com*) allow individuals to shop around on their own and buy their own insurance. And while this can save money, the downside is that you do not have a local agent to help you when problems and accidents arise.

Personally, I prefer having an individual in town that I can go to and will stand up for me if I need assistance with a difficult claim. And I'm in no way suggesting that non-agent companies such as Geico and USAA aren't high quality, reputable companies. I just feel better looking a real human being in the face, shaking their hand, and knowing that when they tell me I'm covered, I am.

Like any other professional, you should expect your agent to meet with you on an annual basis and review your current policy to make sure it's adequate. For example, often people's homes appreciate in value, yet they forget to increase their homeowner's policy to reflect that increase. When that happens and damage occurs to the house, the homeowner may pay a significant amount of the repairs out of pocket because of this oversight. Of course, this kind of personalized service may (but not always) cost a bit more, but you're paying for a higher level of service.

How to Pick a Good Financial Advisor

So what do you do if it's time for a change? Well, if you've decided to fire your current financial advisor and begin looking for someone new, here are a few things that can help you along the way.

1) Get information from the SEC if you're working with a stockbroker

Obviously, you want to have not only a reputable advisor, but one who works for a firm you can trust. The U.S. Securities and Exchange Commission (SEC) protects investors and maintains the integrity of the securities markets, and helps investors like yourself by enforcing federal and state securities laws which require advisors and their firms to be licensed or registered. The SEC also requires that information about any disciplinary action be made public.

The SEC website has investor information with tips on everything from making complaints to explanations of investments to calculators that help with social security and retirement planning. It's available on the web at *http://www.sec.gov*.

Even though the SEC requires information about advisors and firms be available to the public, they do not provide that information themselves. It's up to you to find how your advisor, or a potential advisor, is doing and protect yourself. And in most instances, a phone call or Internet search can help you avoid an unethical advisor or a disreputable firm.

This information is available through the Central Registration Depository (CRD). The CRD is a computer database that contains information about brokers and firms, and it can provide a wealth of information that can help you make the right decision. The CRD will tell you if an advisor is licensed to sell investments in your state, if they have been disciplined by the SEC, and if others investors have filed complaints about the advisor. You'll also learn about the advisor's educational back-ground and other firms he or she has worked for in the past.

2) Check out your broker

As an investor, you can't access the CRD yourself. But there's two ways you can get this information. You can either contact your state securities regulator, or ask the National Association of Securities Dealers, Inc. (NASD) to give you this information.

The best way to find your state securities regulator is through the North American Securities Administrators Association. Their website is http://www.nasaa.org, or you can call them at (202) 737-0900. They can provide contact information for your state's securities regulator, who can look up advisors for you.

Or you can ask the NASD to check out a broker or firm for you. They accept requests through both the Internet and over the phone and are often the fastest and easiest way to get this information. Learn more on the NASD website at http://www.nasdr.com/2000.asp, or call them at (800)289-9999.

3) Find out if your broker is certified

There are several certifications available to advisors, and in order to find a good advisor, you should look for and understand some of the more important ones for your needs.

• _Certified Financial Planner (CFP)_

Although the NASD does not require it, many advi-sors are voluntary certified to meet ethical and edu-cational standards. The Certified Financial Planner Board of Standards (CFP Board) is an organization that encourages advisors to follow professional standards in financial planning. Advisors who meet the CFP Board's qualifications are designated as CFPs, and the title usually appears on the advisor's business card and stationery.

You can learn more, as well as search for CFP-designated advisors, at *http://www.CFP.net*. The CFP Board can also be reached at 888-237-6275.

It's important to understand that although a CFP® designation is a good indicator of overall financial knowledge and background, it doesn't indicate an advisor's expertise of the field in which they've chosen to practice. For example, a CFP certificant may meet the CFP Board's standards and ethics for professionalism, but since the designation does not cover the financial planning needs of seniors, there's no guarantee that a CFP understands or knows about the things we've covered in this book.

• *Certified Senior Advisor (CSA)*

Fortunately, there are designations for planners who work with seniors, such as the Certified Senior Advisor (CSA). The CSA is offered by the Society of Certified Senior Advisors (SOCSA), and in order to earn the certification, an advisor must attend training, learn about the special needs of seniors who invest, and understand the opportunities available to senior citizens. CSAs also adhere to a code of professional responsibility, much like CFP certificants are required to do.

You can learn more, as well as search for CSAs, at *http://www.society-csa.com*. The SOCSA can also be reached at 800-653-1785.

4) **Check out organizations your broker is affiliated with**

Many organizations are specifically designed to help educate and protect seniors during their retirement years. Be sure to check out your broker's affiliations to ensure they have your best interest at heart.

• *National Senior Resource Center (NSRC)*

The National Senior Resource Center is an advocacy organization for persons 55+ working to promote consumer awareness of various issues affecting older adults. The NSRC acts on issues and provides education that meet the greatest community good and will have the biggest impact on those who have retired and continue to actively pursue their goals. To learn more about the National Senior Resource Center, visit *http://www.nationalsrc.com*.

Once you've found the right advisor, you should ask some questions during your first meeting with him or her. Remember that although you want a good advisor, he or she also wants your business. So don't be afraid to treat a meeting with a potential advisor as an interview.

You might want to ask the following:

- What experience do you have helping senior investors like myself?

- Do you work exclusively with seniors?

- What licenses do you hold? Are you registered with the SEC or state?

- What products or services do you offer?

- Do you hold any certifications such as the CSA?

- Have you ever been disciplined or sued by a client who was not happy with your work?

Now that you've determined just what it is you're trying to accomplish and have selected the best advisors and professionals for your needs, let's get into the nitty-gritty of senior planning. In the next chapter we'll discuss one of the best ways to keep the money you've earned from years of hard work – tax planning.

CHAPTER 5

Tax Planning

■■■■■■■■■■■■■■■■■■■■■■■■■■■■■■

"There is nothing sinister in so arranging one's affairs so as to make taxes as low as possible.

"Everybody does so, rich or poor, and do right, for nobody owes any public duty to pay more taxes than the law demands.

"Taxes are enforced exactions, not voluntary contributions."

Justice Learned Hand
United States Appellate Court

■■■■■■■■■■■■■■■■■■■■■■■■■■■■■■

W hen it comes to protecting your piece of the American Dream, the biggest problem all of us face is taxes. We all know that the taxman wants as much money as he can get, and year after year he just keeps on taking from taxpayers. Even worse, if you manage to make more money, the taxman expects you give him even more of it.

It seems that every time we come into contact with money, we're taxed. We pay taxes when we earn it, we pay taxes when we spend it, we pay taxes when we save it, we pay taxes when we give it to someone else, and we're going to pay taxes when we die. Yet what's funny is that our country was founded by people who were tired of paying so many taxes.

A Brief History of the Tax Code

Think about the Boston Tea Party. All that tea was dumped into the Boston harbor because Americans were letting England know that they weren't going to pay taxes on their tea. Our forefathers took a stand against taxation without representation, but look at where we are in the 21st century. Do you believe you're being well represented when it comes to taxes? Did you vote to have your Social Security income taxed? How about the taxes that are added to your cell phone bill? Most people pay a city and state tax just for using a cell phone. You certainly didn't ask for that. Your city and state simply added them on because they decided it was for a good cause.

Until recently, our country had a $3 trillion surplus. Of course, once the economy stumbled and we began the war in Iraq after September 11, 2001, that amount quickly disappeared. Now we have a deficit, and some insist that our taxes are needed to fight the war on terrorism and keep America going. But is that actually true?

About six years ago, I began asking people if they believed that our country's surplus really existed. The vast majority said no, and many thought it was an outright lie. Two things had to exist in order for that surplus to be real. First, we were told that the surplus would exist if we did not have a recession in the next 10 years. Of course, at the time the United States was in the longest economic expansion period of its history, so spending was increasing almost daily. Regardless, everyone will agree that we went into a recession after September 11, 2001.

Secondly, we were told that in order for the surplus to exist, the United States would have to cut its spending by 20% over the next 10 years. Our country has never had a president who left office spending less than when he took office. Many have pointed out that President Reagan spent less during his term in office, but once debt issuances were included this was no longer the case. Most importantly, Congress didn't even include the biggest debt this country has, Social Security, in its supposed surplus.

An article from CBS *MarketWatch* in October 2003 explained these beliefs to be true. At the time, the projected budget deficit for fiscal year 2004 was $600 billion, thanks in part to the war in Iraq. Yet as Bush's term in office continues, we've seen unlimited tax cuts for the ultra-wealthy and limitless spending. By the time our soldiers leave Iraq, who knows what the final tally will be.

The article also mentions some frightening research done by two former presidential economists. According to William Gale, an economist with the senior Bush's Council of Economic Advisors, and Peter Orszag, a special assistant to Clinton on economic policy, our nation has gone from an annual surplus of $127 billion in 2001 to a $300 billion deficit in 2003. These PhD-educated economists also expect the deficit to double in 2004 and have determined that the overall federal account has shifted from a long-term surplus of $5.6 trillion to a deficit of $2.3 trillion.

What's worse, according to Gale and Orszag, is the official numbers used by the government are misleading because they're based on accounting measures that would have made Enron green with envy.

First, the government bases its figures on the assumption that sunset provisions tied to temporary taxes will never occur. In other words, the government expects that current "temporary" taxes will eventually become permanent.

Second, the government assumes that federal spending will equal inflation. As we've seen over the last few years, that's hardly the case. Services already proposed by the current administration will have to be funded at a higher level just to meet their goals in the future.

Lastly, the government is able to make the deficit appear lower because cash flow surpluses from Social Security, Medicare, and federal employee pensions are not included in their accounting methods.

So according to Gale and Orszag, once you discount these kinds of government assumptions, our federal deficit will become $7.8 trillion by 2013 – quite a difference from the $1.4 trillion the government calculates.

Now, imagine what will happen when baby boomers start retiring in the next 10 years. This potential drain on Medicare and Social Security hasn't even been taken into account.

In order to balance the budget, Gale and Orszag insist that Social Security and Medicare spending would have to be cut by 41%. Of course, no politician is ever going to vote for that kind of a cut for Social Security and Medicare, but does that mean you shouldn't worry? Not hardly.

The bottom line is a real surplus never existed, and today we're in a deficit, which means that we all have to pay taxes to fund our military and all this increased spending. But remember the analogy about playing by the rules? Well, if we take a second to look at the rulebook, some of the rules for taxes have changed.

If you haven't read the 2003 tax law changes, you should do so. We were led to believe that the changes lowered our taxes, which is why so many people received $300 to $600 rebates when they filed. The program also abolished estate taxes, which means you no longer have to pay taxes when you die.

All the restructuring that's gone on the past few years is really nothing but congressional tax shenanigans. As usual, the wealthy will pay less in taxes, and who will be asked to pick up the slack? The backbone of this country – middle income America.

As senior investors, your response to these shenanigans should be to develop a tax strategy that takes advantage of these changes and to arrange your affairs properly.

The New York Tycoon

There was once a very wealthy New York tycoon who needed to borrow $10,000 for a trip to Europe. When he went to his bank to borrow the money, the young banker asked the tycoon what he intended to use as collateral for the loan.

"My Rolls Royce is parked outside," he told the young banker. "You're welcome to hold it until I pay you back."

The banker agreed that the car would suffice, so he took the tycoon's keys and placed the Rolls Royce in a secured garage to protect it from damage and theft. Once it was securely parked, the banker finished the loan, and the tycoon left with his $10,000.

Two weeks later, the tycoon returned from his trip and went to the bank. "I've come back to pay off my loan and get my car back," he told the young banker.

"Of course," the banker responded. As the two were finishing up the loan paperwork, the banker had the Rolls Royce brought from the secure garage. "I must admit that I'm confused," he told the tycoon. "When filling out the paperwork for the loan, I did a credit check on you and found out that you're worth more than $30 million. With so much money, why did you need to borrow $10,000?"

"Where else in Manhattan can you park your car in a secure garage for $37 a week," the tycoon laughed.

The tycoon wasn't breaking the rules by borrowing money to park his car; instead, he was using them to his advantage. He's a perfect example of someone who knows the rulebook and uses it in his favor.

When it comes to taxes, this is what you should strive to do. In fact, it's possible for many senior investors to lower their tax bracket to under 4% by using just a few techniques. It may sound too good to be true, but everything we'll discuss in this chapter is absolutely legal. This is not about offshore trusts or tax dodging schemes, but applying 30-year-old tax strategies to your investments – most likely things that no one has ever gone over with you.

Take another look at the quote in the beginning of this chapter. Judge Hand basically said that as U.S. citizens, we're allowed to arrange our affairs in order to pay the least amount in taxes legally possible. In fact, he said it's our duty to do so. After all, isn't this what our country was founded on?

I'm proud to be an American and willing to pay my fair share of taxes, as long as our government gives something in return such as improved roads, better schools, and military defense. But our government also wastes an awful lot of money, which it gets from our hard earned dollars. And you and I can be just as proud of America for half as much money. Don't you agree?

A Tax on a Tax

While there are some taxes you can't do anything about, there are four taxes that you can significantly reduce with a little bit of simple planning. You can reduce taxes on your interest and dividends, you can reduce taxes on your capital gains, you can reduce or eliminate taxes on your death, and many senior investors can reduce or eliminate taxes on Social Security income.

Social Security is one of the most important areas to address when looking at your tax situation. Because really, taxes on your Social Security income is a tax on a tax. Social Security was a tax you were forced to pay for years, and now you're still taxed when you get that money back. The government gets you coming and going, doesn't it?

Several times a year, I attend symposiums for the financial services industry. And at these gatherings, I ask my fellow associates what they're doing about their clients' Social Security tax.

"Nothing," they always tell me. "It's no big deal." Of course, they say that because it's not a big deal to them. But 20 or 30 years from now they'll have a different answer. And any advisor who thinks this way does not have your best interests at heart.

As you know, FDR created Social Security back in 1935, and three years later people started receiving benefits. At the time, the U.S. Treasury said that Social Security was a gift and that it would never be taxed. Well, to be honest, it wasn't a gift in the first place. Since when do you have to pay for a gift?

But even though FDR promised that Social Security would never be taxed, look at what's happened. And it's not surprising. After all, what do politicians find easy to make, but hard to keep? Promises.

Unlike most politicians, FDR kept his promise. But in 1983, Congress created a law that allowed 50% of your Social Security income to be taxed. To make matters worse, Congress increased that amount to 85% in 1993. And it won't be long before Congress decides it's okay to tax that last 15%.

When you worked, did you and your fellow employees meet in a back room once a year to vote yourselves raises? That's what Congress does. Every year, members of Congress meet, and despite current layoffs, a bad job market, and people with little money to spend, Congress gives itself an increase in salary. It usually happens on a Saturday night, so that it attracts little attention in the Sunday newspaper, and by Monday, other news has made people forget all about it.

Factor in that most members of Congress are either millionaires or owe their election to gifts from millionaires, and they have little incentive to lower taxes on Social Security income. Since it doesn't affect them, why should they care?

If you own tax-free municipal bonds, you may already realize that they're not really tax-free. When you file your 1040 every year, you have to report any tax free interest you receive, which includes these bonds. So if these bonds are truly tax-free, why are

> If you own tax-free municipal bonds, you may already realize that they're not really tax-free.

you required to report the interest? Because they are taxed when you begin receiving Social Security.

In fact, municipal bonds are the only investment that cannot qualify for a long-term gains rate. When a municipal bond bought at a discount matures at face value, the investor is required to pay taxes on the difference. If the discount price of the bond was less than 0.25% of the face value for each full year remaining until maturity, the gain qualifies for exemption to the discount rule and is taxed as a capital gain. Worse yet, if the discount exceeds this level, the entire gain is taxed at the higher ordinary income rate.

As you can see, tax-free municipal bonds are tax-free for people in their 20's, 30's, 40's, and 50's. But for seniors? No way. You're taxed when you draw Social Security. Washington continues to treat the Greatest Generation poorly, and that's a crime.

I once met a woman who exemplified this perfectly. She had an appointment with me, and as she introduced herself, she was feeling very proud because her broker had put her in $250,000 of municipal bonds. The woman took out her statement and showed it to me, and I said, "Oh, I'm sorry."

"What do you mean?" she said. I asked if I could see her tax return, and when she showed it to me, I immediately saw that those $250,000 of municipal bonds were causing her to pay an additional $3,000 a year in taxes.

Talk about killing the messenger! Once I explained this to her, I was barely able to get her out of the office while I was still alive. Apparently, the truth *does* hurt.

It was obvious that her broker had never looked at the woman's tax return. So do you think her broker ever explained to her that her tax-exempt bonds could be taxable? Absolutely not.

This can be confusing if you don't understand how Social Security is taxed. So if you want to know just how much of your

Social Security is being taxed, get your most recent 1040 and do the following:

1. Add lines 8a and 9 (interest and dividends)

2. Add line 8b (tax-free income)

3. Add line 13 (capital gains)

4. Add line 16 (pension income)

5. Add your other income from all sources

6. If you're married and earn more than $32,000, or single and earn more than $25,000, add 50% of your Social Security income.

   If you're married and earn more than $44,000, or single and earn more than $34,000, add 85% of your Social Security income.

This total is your provisional income, and the IRS uses this number to determine how much of your Social Security income is taxed. So as you can see, the tax on your Social Security is based on a lot more than just your Social Security income.

The Good Steward is Punished

Do you see how the system is designed to work against you? It's frustrating, because not only did your generation build this county, but you were also good savers. You believed that "a penny saved is a penny earned" and trusted the motto "waste not, want not." Your taxes made Social Security what it is today; yet instead of being thanked and rewarded for your efforts, you're being taxed. Quite simply, you are a generation of good stewards who are being punished for your hard work.

On top of this, each year the tax bracket goes up a little bit for each rate. All the brackets are adjusted for inflation, which means the income bracket making up the 15% tax bracket goes up a little bit, the income needed to reach the 28% tax bracket goes up a little bit, and so does the income needed to reach all the others.

Your deductions are also indexed for inflation. So are your exemptions. In fact, everything is indexed for inflation except for, you guessed it, Social Security.

This means that since the IRS started taxing Social Security in 1983, they have not indexed any of those brackets for inflation.

Of course, in 1983, $32,000 was a pretty darn good income. At the time, the average income was $21,073 a year, homes cost an average of $82,600, and the average car cost $8,577. Then again, that was 20 years ago. What is $32,000 going to get you today? Not much.

So when Congress and politicians tell you that they're going to help you reduce your taxes, you should be skeptical. After all, how much have the recent tax breaks helped you? Probably not much. Do you think you're going to be getting a lot of tax breaks from those tax cuts? No.

The most important issue of our last presidential election was prescriptions. You probably remember all the news stories about seniors taking buses to Mexico and Canada to get their prescriptions filled. And I don't blame them. If you can save money, do it.

The second most important issue of the election was Social Security, and the third most important issue was Medicare. The fourth most important issue was education. Do you know where taxes ranked on this list of important issues?

The Bottom Line

So although Congress insisted they were going to do this really big favor for us, they turned around and ignored all the issues we said were important to us. What did they do instead? They sent us a $300 or $600 check.

But what's really upsetting is that seniors are the most influential group of voters in this country. The AARP has more clout on Capitol Hill than anyone else, and no politician in their right mind would speak out against the AARP. But we still got hoodwinked by those tax rebate checks, which they did so we'd leave them alone.

The bottom line is the same as it's always been. The people who benefit the most from the recent tax law changes are the very wealthy. The vast majority of middle-class, hardworking people in this country will not benefit from these tax law changes, yourself included.

So, how do you get a tax break? You become informed.

How Your Investments are Taxed

Now that we've talked about municipal bonds being taxed and reducing your taxes on Social Security, we're going to discuss mutual funds. And when it comes to mutual funds, there are a few key things you need to know.

First, you should understand that all mutual funds must distribute 90% of everything they bring in for capital gains and dividends. If you've owned a mutual fund for more than a year, you'll receive a 1099 for it. This reflects your capital gains and dividends, which means even though you're holding the fund, you still have to pay taxes on it.

Of course, we were all made aware of how much the new tax treatment of dividends was going to help us. Just about everyone in Washington explained time and again that we'd get a huge boon from this change. But in hindsight, who did it really help?

The new tax-favored status is wonderful for the super rich, because all of the shares of DuPont, Exxon, or whatever company from which they receive dividends puts them in the tax bracket of a waitress. On the other hand, the middle-class, which owns mutual funds instead of millions in company stock, were once again taken to the cleaners. This is because mutual funds pay the internal fees using dividends first, which means the tax-favored status of dividends is gobbled up by fund fees. As a result, you won't ever receive the tax advantage from this status.

Depending on your experience with mutual funds, you may or may not know what a turnover ratio is. Turnover ratio is a statistical way of saying how many stocks are bought and sold by a mutual fund. For example, let's say you own a mutual fund that invests in 100 different stocks, and that fund has an annual turnover ratio of 94%. This means that out of those 100 stocks, the fund manager is going to sell 94 of them this year, and replace each of those with a different stock.

By today's standards, a turnover ratio of 110% is considered average. Yet 10 years ago, the average turnover ratio was only 24%. Each year this ratio has gone up, and some fund managers are selling and buying stocks as if they were day traders. I've seen mutual funds with a 400% turnover ratio. This means that if the fund has 100 stocks, the fund manager will sell all 100 stocks, then replace them with something different. And he's going to do it again, and again, and again. In other words, he's going to sell every stock in the fund an average of four times over the course of just one year. Each stock in the fund would be held for an average of just three months.

And if you own a mutual fund with a high turnover ratio, you can imagine what it would do to your tax situation. Every time the manager sold a stock, he or she would have capital gains to contend with. And we said a moment ago, 90% of all capital gains must be distributed – which means they give them to you, and you end up paying taxes on them.

Of course, fund managers who buy and sell stocks on a constant basis do so to improve the funds returns and capital gains. And that's not such a bad thing – except when it comes to taxes.

Look at it this way: when you sell a stock within 12 months of buying it, the stock is considered short-term. And when you sell a stock more than 12 months after buying it, the stock is considered long-term. As you know, short-term gains are much worse for taxes than long-term gains. In fact, short-term gains mean you'll pay anywhere from a 33% to 50% more in taxes than you would for long-term gains.

So if a manager is churning stocks inside a mutual fund, the tax treatment of that fund is going to be extremely poor. But your advisor may not be telling you that.

Another issue that affects taxes of mutual funds is which shares are sold and when. Anyone that's done capital gains for their taxes is familiar with the different kinds of record keeping the IRS will accept. There's FIFO, or "First In, First Out," which is the most expensive way of handling capital gains, and there's HIFO, or "Highest In, First Out," which means that selling the highest-priced shares of that company, regardless of when you purchased them.

For example, let's say you've bought some shares of XYZ stock at $10, some more at $20, and some more at $30. Now you want to sell some of those shares, and the going price is $40 a share. You'd want to sell the shares using HIFO, which would give you a minimal gain of $10 on each share. If you sold the same number of shares using FIFO, you'd see a gain of $30 per share, and you'd pay more in taxes, even though you'd receive the same amount for your sale. That's a huge difference!

Most people who don't know better, or haven't kept good records, determine their gains by using the FIFO method. But as you can see, those who take the time to keep track of their sales often use the HIFO method and save themselves a lot of money on capital gains taxes in the process. The IRS doesn't care which method you use, as long as you're consistent and your records support the method you use.

Well, mutual funds are just like individual investors when it comes to their capital gains. Some go to the trouble of keeping good records and using the HIFO method to save money on capital gains, while other funds don't worry about it and are forced to use the FIFO method. About an equal number of funds use each method, meaning there's a 50/50 split between users of FIFO and HIFO.

Mutual Fund magazine once asked funds that use FIFO why they didn't use the HIFO method, since it would save money on capital gains. The majority of fund companies replied that it was just too much work to keep track of.

It's easy to say something is too much work when someone else has to deal with the repercussions of the situation. So while funds may not think it's important to bother with using HIFO, you'll pay the price for their laziness – in extra taxes.

By far, one of the most frustrating things about mutual funds is phantom income. This occurs when you lose money on a mutual fund, but still get a 1099 for it because of gains on individual stocks. A few years ago, this was almost unheard of. But today, it's becoming a common occurrence. If you want to avoid phantom income, watch your fund's capital gains and turnover ratio.

Even if you ignore the tax issues, high turnover rates are still a bad thing. Let's say that a fund manager sells off $30 million of a particular stock in his fund. When someone sells that much of one company, the stock price usually goes down in response. So at this point, let's assume the fund holds $29 million in cash. Now let's say the manager uses that cash to purchase a new stock. And when someone purchases that much of one company, the price of the stock goes up. So at this point, the fund has bought $28 million of the new company's stock.

In other words, the fund started out with $30 million of one stock, and replaced it with $28 million of another stock. When this happens, the fund has to recoup that two million just to get even, which means the fund manager now has to take more risk in the market to cover his loss. So essentially, the higher the turnover ratio, the riskier that fund is.

By the way, isn't it interesting that advisors tell us to buy and hold stocks, then turn right around and suggest funds where the managers are churning through stocks on almost a daily basis? It's as if what's good for the goose isn't good for the gander. So if you're a buy-and-hold investor, you owe it to yourself to make sure your funds are buy-and-hold as well. And the best way to find this out is by comparing turnover ratios.

The bottom line is that you should take the time to learn about your funds and understand that not all funds are created equal. CNNfn says that one of the darkest secrets of the mutual fund industry is that taxes can wipe out a significant chunk of your investment returns. Neil Wolfson, a tax expert with accounting firm KPMG, says most investors have been in the dark about mutual funds. He believes the majority of investors remain woefully uniformed about the tax implications of a fund manager's trading decisions. And not surprisingly, Joel Dickson, a Vanguard Group principal, says that while there are thousands of funds, only 30 or so are tax-managed. So if your fund has a high turnover ratio, you could be writing a big check to Uncle Sam.

It's very easy to determine or find the turnover ratio of a fund, and if your advisor can't do that for you, you should ask yourself whether he or she is looking out for you or themselves.

Above all, make sure you know not just the fund's rate of return, but your rate of return net of taxes. What matters is not how much money the fund makes, but how much money you make.

What Can You Do?

The most important thing you can do is stop paying taxes on money you're not spending. Of course, if you are spending your money, good for you. You've worked hard for it, so spend it and enjoy yourself. But if you're not spending money, don't pay taxes on it.

The best way to do this is by positioning your money in investments where taxes are handled on a deferred basis. Some investors disagree, and you might be rolling your eyes right now. "That's a problem waiting to happen," is a common response. "I'm going to have to pay taxes on it eventually, so why not just pay now?"

Because paying now is actually more costly than deferring your taxes. Look at the following example:

Let's say that you have a tax bill of $2,700 per year, but you've decided to defer it for 10 years. So you defer $2,700 in year one and another $2,700 in year two, and you continue to do this for 10 years. Now during this time, you continue to earn 6% interest. At the end of those 10 years, your $2,700 has grown to $36,000 thanks to your investments.

Of course, you still have to pay taxes on it, which means Uncle Sam could take up to one-third of your $36,000, or $12,000, depending on your tax bracket. But even though you just paid the IRS $12,000, you've netted an additional $24,000 by deferring your taxes.

But compare this to your grumpy old friend who said you were being a fool. He was in the same situation and decided to pay his taxes each year. He pays $2,700 in the first year, another $2,700 in the second year, and so on for the next 10 years. Once everything is done, your friend has paid $27,000 in taxes over the course of those 10 years, and he doesn't keep anything.

No one in their right mind wants to end up with nothing when they can end up with $24,000. So don't pay taxes on money you're not spending.

We all would like more income and fewer taxes, and you can have your cake and eat it too if you take advantage of two provisions in the tax code. IRS Reg 1.72–2(b) and IRS code section 72(b)(1) can help. These are called exclusion ratios and can be used to create a split tax plan that will reduce tax on your income. The difference is these exclusion ratios are contrary to that old idea of spend your interest but save your principal. We've all learned this, but in order to take advantage of these provisions, you'll have to think differently.

These provisions provide a way to arrange your affairs so that you pay 1.5% tax on your income instead of paying up to 34% in tax. They allow you to increase your income while reducing your taxes and may cut your taxes on capital gains in half. You probably aren't familiar with this, but don't you think you should be?

Understanding Taxes as it Pertains to the Retired Person

In order to understand how taxes are affecting you, it's necessary to look at your annual tax return in light of your investments. So while your accountant may handle your tax return and your advisor may handle your portfolio, these documents need to be compared to each other.

The first step is for you and your advisor to go through your tax return every year. Schedule an appointment, and sit down with them to review your 1040. If your advisor is on the ball, there are several areas he or she may be able to help you with.

Begin by looking at lines 8a and 8b. There's probably income you could defer. For example, do you have income from municipal bonds? If so, it's causing you to pay increased taxes on your Social Security. Also, look at line 9 for help with sheltering dividends. Look at line 12 if you own your own business and line 13 for help in reducing capital gains. Line 16 will help with your exclusion ratio, and line 20b will tell you how much your Social Security is being taxed.

Most municipal bonds aren't taxed for federal purposes, but they can be taxed for social security purposes, depending on your income. Federal bonds, on the other hand, are taxed for federal purposes and Social Security, but not for state purposes.

If you are reinvesting interest from savings bonds, annuities or the cash value on your life insurance, you won't pay federal, state or Social Security tax.

The point is that you need to fully explore all your choices for reinvested taxable money. You should not pay taxes on money that is growing and that you're not spending.

Of course, if you're comfortable with how much you're paying in taxes each April, don't worry about it. Some people such as Ross Perot put all their money in municipal bonds and don't worry about taxes on social security. But the rest of us who aren't rich could stand to use some help.

What About Annuities in My IRA?

Although there are a variety of tools to defer taxes, annuities are the most popular way to do so. But not all annuities are good, and you need to be cautious of insurance companies and agents when considering these products.

Many annuity companies lure investors with a high interest rate for the first year, but lower it to sub par levels once the interest rate renews in the second year. Like many senior investors, you may have realized this too late. Many of you opened up annuities years ago and are no longer happy with your current interest rates. You realize that other companies pay higher interest rates, but you're concerned that if you move your money, you'll have to pay taxes on it.

But if you're in this situation, there's good news. IRS code section 1035 allows you to refinance old annuities so you can get a higher interest rate. The section allows you to move your annuity to a new company without having to pay any taxes.

Another concern is penalties. Some companies require investors to pay a surrender penalty if they transfer their money to a different annuity. Fortunately, there is a handful of companies with high interest rates that will pay your surrender penalty for you.

So if your annuity is low interest, you owe it to yourself to shop around for a better interest rate and to refinance it when you find one. If you're currently getting 3% from your annuity instead of shopping for a rate of 4.5% to 6%, you're letting your insurance company earn extra money off your investment. And most of us aren't so generous as to give large corporations an extra bit of our money.

If your annuity is low-interest, you owe it to yourself to shop around for a better interest rate…

And although we've discussed the benefits of tax-deferral, there's something even better – paying no tax at all. What if your insurance company agreed to pay the taxes for you upon your death? It would certainly save your children and spouse a lot of headache, not to mention money. Some annuities realize this, and there are a handful of companies that pay an extra 28% to 40% on your gains to cover the taxes associated with them.

Many senior investors say, "We've done a good job providing for our kids. We sent them to a good college and gave them good values, so they're entitled to whatever is left over after taxes. But only after we're done with it ourselves." There's nothing wrong with that, but if you're concerned about the amount of taxes your children will pay once you're gone, there are companies out there that will pay them. You just need to find those companies and start investing with them.

But before you start moving your money around, remember this: not all annuities are good. In fact, brokers often put variable annuities inside an IRA, something you should avoid at all costs. The National Association of Securities Dealers (NASD) is the policing agency that watches over securities dealers, and even they're against it. The NASD issues and revokes licenses, as well as fines dealers who break the law, and in 1999 they put out a Notice (# 99-35) stating that a variable annuity inside of an IRA is almost never a good thing. The notice also stresses that the person who puts money into these kinds of investments should have an extremely strong and compelling reason for doing so. Yet more and more brokers are pushing this very concept.

So if a variable annuity is inside your IRA, ask your advisor why. If they can't give you a perfect reason for this, you're flushing 5% to 20% of your annual return down the toilet. And as with low interest rates, you're simply giving away more of your hard-earned money.

Another major problem with variable annuities is what's called Income Benefit Riders. These promise the investor a supposed 6% or 7% guaranteed interest rate. The problem with these riders is that in order to get the 6% to 7% interest rate, you're required to turn over all your money to the insurance company, leaving you with nothing. In turn, they pay you an income based on a return of only 1.5% for the rest of your life. Obviously, that's not a 6% or 7% guarantee.

Are B Shares Okay to Own in a Mutual Fund?

Another significant problem is Class B shares inside of mutual funds. This has become a fairly regular problem, and many people say they bought Class B shares because they are no-load as long as they stay in the fund for six or seven years.

Yet that's not true. B shares are loaded with 12(b)-1 fees, although most people don't realize it. These 12(b)-1 fees are disclosed inside of the prospectus for B shares, but most investors overlook it or don't read the prospectus at all. So if your mutual fund has B shares, look at the prospectus, because it's in there. And if you're paying 12(b)-1 fees in your mutual fund, you're probably being overcharged roughly 1% a year for the six or seven years they're in the fund.

Let's say that you have $85,000 in your IRA, and your spouse has $55,000 in his or her IRA. The two of you have well over $100,000 combined in your IRAs, and if both of them have B shares, you're paying a lot of money for that privilege. It's just more money you're giving away.

Let me explain why this happens. Owning B shares is like buying an egg from a farmer for $0.25, then coming back a week later to buy 1,000 eggs. If you return to buy that many eggs, you must really like them. Well, the farmer will appreciate the fact that you're willing to buy so many eggs at one time, so he'll probably give you a break on the price. More than likely, you'd end up paying much less than $0.25 for each egg because you're buying so many.

Mutual funds work the same way. Companies have to give you break points and lower your initial sales cost if you invest a certain value in the fund.

Most of the time, advisors put investors into B shares rather than A shares because it means more money for them. This has become such a huge problem that the Securities and Exchange Commission (SEC) has said that every salesperson should disclose and keep records of available break points.

Yet the vast majority of people who own B shares do not know about break-points. If an advisor recommends B shares over A shares, but does not give any proof of how this benefits the customer, disciplinary action could be taken against the advisor. So you need to be aware of variable annuities inside of your IRA, as well as B shares inside your mutual fund.

What to do With all that IRA and 401(k) Money

Thirty years ago, the biggest asset most people in the United States owned was their house. Today, it's their IRA. And like most senior investors, you've probably accumulated quite a bit of money in your IRA. It's a great deal, but once you start pulling money out of it, you have to pay taxes on it.

Of course, we'd all like to take money out of our IRA without paying taxes on it. The problem is that's just not possible. But the way to use the system to your benefit is to take your money out in a tax-efficient manner.

One of the things you can do is take advantage of IRS section 42. It's run by the US Treasury, and it's called a tax credit program or tax forgiveness program.

Here's how it works: Let's say you've taken $10,000 out of your IRA, and that withdrawal results in $3,000 of taxes. You can't do anything about that $3,000 in taxes, but what if you have some tax credits? Suppose you've arranged your assets in such a way that they've created $3,000 in tax credits for yourself. If so, you may owe $3,000 in taxes for your IRA withdrawal, but you've also been forgiven $3,000 in taxes. In this situation, your net tax change on your return is zero. With just a little planning and timing, you've effectively pulled $10,000 out of your IRA without any additional tax burden.

Now, there are some advantages and disadvantages to this program, but you won't be able to weigh the pros and cons of this unless someone explains it to you. The only way to decide if this tax credit program is good for you is to discuss it with your advisor. Of course, your advisor has to know about it and understand it in order to help you. So if they don't, ask yourself why they haven't told you about it already. You deserve to be aware of every option available.

Would you also like to increase the value of your IRA by 300% or more? Obviously we'd all like to do that! The catch is that this isn't for you, but your beneficiaries – it benefits your kids and grandkids.

There is a provision in the tax code that allows you to defer taxation of your IRA for up to two generations. For example, let's say that at your death, your spouse inherits your IRA and defers the taxes over his or her lifetime. But once your spouse dies and your children or grandkids inherit your IRA, they'll have to pay the taxes on it within one to five years. More importantly, they stand to lose up to 50% to 70% of the IRA due to taxes.

Instead of leaving your children and grandchildren with this burden, you could decide to create a "stretch IRA." This would allow your kids and grandkids to defer taxes on the balance of your IRA so they can create a consistent income over their lifetime.

With a stretch IRA, your beneficiaries can turn a modest account of thousands into millions by deferring taxes on it instead of paying the taxes within one to five years. And should your kids or grandkids want to accelerate the distribution or take it all out right away, they can do that as well. Or if you're worried that your 21-year-old grandson will blow it all during his first year of college, you can limit the distribution so it comes out slowly over time.

This can literally turn an IRA into millions of dollars and create a lifetime income and a family legacy while saving tens of thousands in taxes. The stretch IRA is simple to implement, but you need to put the proper paperwork in place now. So if you're interested, ask your advisor if this is appropriate for you.

By the way, 401(k)s and 403(b)s are not allowed this treatment, so if you own one of these investments, get in touch with a qualified senior advisor as soon as possible.

The Roth IRA

A few years ago, Congress created the Roth IRA. As you probably know, the great thing about Roth IRAs is that they grow tax- free throughout your lifetime and your spouse's lifetime. But did you know you could extend that? If you combine a Roth IRA with a stretch IRA, it will be tax-free not only in your and your spouse's lives, but also throughout your children's and grandchildren's lives as well if set up properly.

But there's a problem. If you convert a traditional IRA to a Roth IRA, you have to pay the conversion tax up front. When the Roth IRA first started, you were able to spread out the conversion taxes over four years – but not any more. So if you move $100,000 from your regular IRA to your Roth IRA, you'll have to pay somewhere around $30,000 in taxes, and that amount will be due as soon as you move it.

But as with any problem, there's a solution. In this situation, you could utilize a little-known tax option that allows you to take a discount on the conversion of up to 59%. How? By utilizing the Tiered Retirement Equity Enhancement Program. And although you're probably not aware of this, your advisor should be. Wouldn't you prefer to pay tax on only 41% of your IRA, as compared to all of it?

Tiered Retirement Equity Enhancement for IRAs

- Pulls out up to 59% of your IRA tax-free.

- Reduces your taxes by 50%.

- Guarantees that you cannot run out of money.

- Works by using the tax code in your favor (IRS Sec. 1.401(a)(9) 6 and Sec. 54.4974-2).

These kinds of tax solutions can make a big difference in your federal income tax, but you need your advisor's input and advice to determine which of these products will help you write a smaller check to Uncle Sam each April. And that means your advisor should look over your tax return.

Once you reduce the tax on your Social Security income, it's savings that you never have to pay back. And isn't that the best reason to do these things?

Why Aren't My Advisor and Accountant Telling Me This Stuff?

A lot of people ask, "Why hasn't my CPA told me about all this?" It's a fair question and one I'd ask if I learned I could save money on taxes.

Whenever you file your taxes, be it a 1040 or other form, there are two signature lines. One is for you, and the other is for your tax preparer (not tax advisor, tax *preparer*). You're paying this individual to look over last year's information, plug in the correct numbers, do all the math, and keep you out of trouble. You're not paying a tax preparer for advice, although many people make the mistake of believing they are.

As you probably realize, tax preparers make most of their money during the months of February, March, and April. This is because it's "tax season," and they're preparing tons of tax returns. And they know that the more people they file taxes for, the more money they make.

Now, imagine that it's March 20, and your preparer is swamped with clients and tax forms to complete. It's three in the morning, and they're burning the midnight oil when the preparer begins working on your form.

"You know what," they say to themselves, "I think Mr. Smith could benefit from this tax-reduction strategy. But I'm not sure about all the details, so I'd better grab a few books and do some research to make sure. It shouldn't take more than a couple of hours to figure out. If I'm still not sure, I can always go online and probably figure it out with some additional research."

What's the likelihood of that happening? Not much. Your preparer is paid to prepare your taxes, not save you money in the process. And when time is precious during tax season, your preparer is concerned with getting your form done and moving on to the next client, not looking out for you.

Now I have nothing against accountants. In fact, I have a very good one, and I could not live without him. But, I certainly don't rely on him to reduce my tax bill. It's not his job. You are responsible for lowering your tax bill, and if you need help, you should ask your financial advisor – not your tax preparer.

If you are not doing these things with your advisor every year, then you have to ask yourself why not. Either your advisor doesn't know how to help you or he or she doesn't care. And in my book, it doesn't matter which is true. If they can't help me, I need to find someone who can.

Everyone's different when it comes to how much they can save in taxes. My personal record is saving a client $24,000 a year. That's $240,000 over 10 years. How great would that be?

That's the high end of the scale though. Most of my clients fall in the $2,000 to $4,000 range when it comes to annual tax savings. But even so, imagine what you could do with an extra $2,000 to $4,000 per year. That's $20,000 to $40,000 in ten years. These things we're talking about are worth tens of thousands of dollars in the long run. You could buy a new car with those savings or pay for a grandchild's college education.

Of course, who's really paying for that car or your grandchild's college? The IRS, because it's money you would have had to pay them otherwise. So take advantage of your situation and be informed.

As we have discussed in this chapter, you should recognize that you need to *find* a problem before it *becomes* one. You've also learned that municipal bonds aren't tax-free if you're in the middle-income category and are drawing Social Security. You've learned about the tax problems with mutual funds – things like turnover ratio and phantom income. You've learned how to stretch your beneficiaries and why you should consider a painless Roth IRA. You've learned about the strength of tax-deferral.

You've also learned about insurance companies that pay taxes for you and why you should not have variable annuities inside your IRA. And you've learned about the problems with B shares and why having more than $100,000 in them means you're overpaying. But most importantly, you've learned that if your financial advisor is not telling you about these things, it's because either he or she doesn't know about them or simply doesn't care. And if you're in that situation, you need to find one who does.

So no matter what your financial situation, there's something in this chapter you can use. Next, we're going to look at long-term care planning.

CHAPTER 6

Long-Term
Care Planning

L et's now shift gears and take a look at the fastest growing segment of the population: people 85 and older. Of course, every senior investor knows about long-term care and what it entails. But should you need long-term care, who's going to pay for it?

A year of long-term care can easily cost $40,000 to $50,000, which isn't small potatoes. Think your health insurance will cover everything? Think again and read your policy. Think your HMO will cover you? It won't. Think Medicare will cover you? It will, for the first 20 days. After that, you're on your own.

You may not realize it, but long-term care is the greatest unfunded liability in America. So who pays for it? Well, if we break it down, 4% of LTC coverage is paid by friends or family, while only 5% is paid by LTC insurance. Thirty-one percent of LTC costs are paid by the individual receiving the care, while 12 % is paid by Medicare for the first 20 days someone spends in a nursing home. Lastly,

Medicaid pays for 48% of the cost.

So the two biggest payers of long-term care are the individuals needing LTC and Medicaid. You can imagine what kind of impact this has on a senior's finances and investments. After all, people who need Medicaid to cover their long-term care certainly didn't start out in that situation. In order to qualify for Medicaid, you pretty much have to spend all your money and go broke.

Have you or someone you know ever written a monthly check for the long-term care of a loved one? It's staggering. There are individuals who regularly write out monthly checks for $4,000, $4,200, $5,200, even $5,500. That's for one month of long-term care—just 30 days.

Now imagine how long your nest egg would last if you had to write checks of that size every month. You may have spent 40 years building up your savings, but you could lose it all in a few years.

Listen to what others are saying: According to *Business Week* magazine, nursing home care can blow apart the retirement saved through the years. The *Atlanta Journal* says that the quickest way for your family to lose your property, possessions and money is not to do estate planning. The AARP says that long-term care costs $50,000 a year, and with an average annual inflation of 5%, long-term care costs will rise to $81,445 per year in 10 years. Lastly, the American Health Care Association says that failure to prepare for the cost of long-term care is the primary cause of poverty among the elderly.

Who Needs It?

You do! The majority of seniors in this country are not only gambling with their investments, but with their health as well. And if you don't have long-term care insurance, you're also gambling with your future. Are you willing to risk everything you've worked and saved for in hopes that you won't ever need long-term care?

About half of those reading this book will spend less than $100,000 in long-term care. They're the lucky ones. About 17% of readers will spend somewhere between $100,000 and $500,000 on long-term care. That may seem like a lot, but 8% of those reading this book will spend more than $500,000 on long-term care. That's half a million dollars. And if you don't have the money for long-term care, the government will cover the cost for you, but only after you reach the poverty level by spending all your life savings. Of course, there's no way of knowing which of these categories you'll fall in, and since none of us know how much we'll spend in long-term care, we can do one of two things – either cross our fingers or get long-term care insurance.

Obviously, you don't want to be one of those people who spend a half-a-million dollars on long-term care or go broke trying. No one does. But statistics show that 8% of seniors will spend just that much. So it's better to plan for long-term care and purchase LTC insurance than to hope for the best and cross your fingers. If you don't, you'll be in the government's hands, and we've already seen how poorly they look out for us when it comes to taxes.

Who Sells It and Why?

On average, about 10% of the country has bought long-term care insurance. Of course, more people are buying long-term care insurance each day, but that 10% remains constant because more people are aging while others who own LTC insurance are dying.

The other 90% of the population has long-term care insurance through the government, and if you think that's enough, take a look at how it works.

What will your state let you keep? (as of 7/04)

State	Your Asset Allowance	Spouse's Minimum Asset Allowance	Your Monthly Needs Allowance	Spouse's Monthly Income Allowance
Alabama*	$2,000	$25,000	$30	$1,561
Alaska*	$2,000	$92,760	$75	$2,319
Arizona*	$2,000	$18,552	$82.80	$2,319
Arkansas*	$2,000	$18,552	$40	$1,561
California	$2,000	$92,760	$35	$2,319
Colorado*	$2,000	$92,760	$50	$1,561
Connecticut	$1600	$18,552	$56	$1,561
Delaware*	$2,000	$25,000	$44	$1,561
DC	$2,600	$92,760	$70	$2,319
Florida*	$2,000	$92,760	$35	$1,561
Georgia	$2,000	$92,760	$30	$2,319
Hawaii	$2,000	$92,760	$30	$2,319
Idaho*	$2,000	$18,552	$40	$1,561
Illinois	$2,000	$92,760	$30	$2,319
Indiana	$1,500	$18,552	$52	$1,561
Iowa*	$2,000	$24,000	$30	$2,319
Kansas	$2,000	$18,552	$30	$1,561
Kentucky	$2,000	$22,000	$40	$1,561
Louisiana*	$2,000	$92,760	$38	$2,319
Maine	$2,000	$92,760	$40	$1,561
Maryland	$2,500	$18,552	$50	$1,561
Massachusetts	$2,000	$92,760	$60	$1,561
Michigan	$2,000	$18,552	$60	$1,561
Minnesota	$3,000	$25,247	$72	$1,561
Mississippi*	$2,000	$92,760	$44	$2,319
Missouri	$1,000	$18,552	$30	$1,561
Montana	$2,000	$18,552	$40	$1,561
Nebraska	$4,000	$18,552	$50	$2,319
Nevada*	$2,000	$18,552	$35	$1,561
New Hampshire	$2,500	$18,552	$50	$1,561
New Jersey	$2,000	$18,552	$35	$1,561
New Mexico*	$2,000	$31,290	$49	$1,561
New York	$3,850	$74,820	$50	$2,319
North Carolina	$2,000	$18,552	$30	$1,561
North Dakota	$3,000	$92,760	$50	$2,319
Ohio	$1,500	$18,552	$40	$1,561
Oklahoma*	$2,000	$25,000	$50	$2,319
Oregon*	$2,000	$18,552	$30	$1,561

State	Your Asset Allowance	Spouse's Minimum Asset Allowance	Your Monthly Needs Allowance	Spouse's Monthly Income Allowance
Pennsylvania	$2,400	$18,552	$30	$1,561
Rhode Island	$4,000	$18,552	$50	$1,561
South Carolina*	$2,000	$66,480	$30	$1,662
South Dakota*	$2,000	$20,000	$30	$1,561
Tennessee	$2,000	$18,552	$30	$1,561
Texas*	$2,000	$18,552	$60	$2,319
Utah	$2,000	$18,552	$45	$1,561
Vermont	$2,000	$92,760	$47.66	$1,561
Virginia	$2,000	$18,552	$30	$1,561
Washington	$2,000	$40,000	$41.62	$1,561
West Virginia	$2,000	$18,552	$50	$1,561
Wisconsin	$2,000	$50,000	$45	$1,935
Wyoming*	$2,000	$92,760	$50	$2,319

* These are "income cap" states. If your income is higher than $1,692 a month, you cannot qualify for Medicaid even after spending down all assets, unless you set up a Miller trust. For updated figures, go to http://www.ltcconsultants.com/consumer/wyslyk/index.shtml.

The government will pay for your long-term care only if you meet certain criteria, which means you must have exhausted every financial asset you own before they chip in a cent — and that literally means everything.

For example, in Minnesota, if you have a spouse, the government will allow you to keep your house until you die. If you're single, you're allowed to keep your house for six months before you must sell it to cover your care. The government also allows you to keep your car and $1,500 in burial funds. If you have a burial trust, you're allowed to put as much as you want into that and keep it, but that money must be used for your burial. If you're single, you can keep $3,000 in cash and investments, and married couples can keep $25,247. Lastly, you're allowed to keep a family bible.

That's it. But you're probably thinking that your life insurance will cover you. It might, but then your spouse and children are left with absolutely nothing. "I've got $250,000 in life insurance," A lot of people say, "So if I go into a long-term care facility, spend a lot of money and die, my wife and children will get the $250,000."

The problem is that's not how the system works. If you need long-term care, the government will require you to spend the cash value of your life insurance before they'll take care of you. So what happens in those situations? You spend all of the cash value of your life insurance on long-term care, and your spouse and children end up with nothing when you're gone.

And the government doesn't make exceptions or loopholes when it comes to long-term care. A prenuptial agreement won't protect your assets. Your 401(k) and other retirement accounts have to be used, as well as things like revocable living trusts. So don't believe that certain investments and shelters will be left alone.

For example, let's say Jim and Mary live in Minnesota and have $300,000 in investments, as well as their house and car. Jim needs long-term care, and Mary is forced to spend $274,753 of their investments before they qualify for any government assistance. Mary still has $25,247 in her investments, but how much piece of mind would she have once her nest egg went from $300,000 to $25,247? Not much, because when you think about it, a few problems or repairs can wipe that out. Mary has to buy a new car because her old one's not reliable, she needs a new furnace for the house, and a storm causes some damage to her home, including some repairs to the roof. A few things like that, and Mary's $25,247 is gone.

But there are things you can do besides buying long-term care insurance. If you're part of that 10% who owns LTC insurance, congratulations. But what about the other 90% of seniors who don't have it?

You can choose to shift the risk to your insurance company. As you may know, LTC insurance is not only expensive, but your premiums will almost assuredly increase. And if you can't afford your premiums 10 years down the road, you'll have to cancel your coverage. What happens then? Well, you certainly don't get your money back. And what happens if you die without ever needing long-term care? Well, your beneficiaries certainly don't get your money. When it comes to long-term care insurance, you either use it or lose it.

10 Secrets Your Long-term Care Salesperson Doesn't Want You to Know

Everyone should have long-term care insurance, but it is expensive and not everyone qualifies because of their health. So if you're thinking about LTC insurance, make sure you protect yourself. The following list will not only make you an informed consumer, but also help you separate the handful of long-term care advisors out there from all the long-term care salespeople you're likely to meet.

1. "Don't ask me this question!"

There's one question every long-term care salesperson doesn't want you to ask:

"What are the last three books you read about long-term care issues?"

You can imagine what you're going to hear. "Well, I went through the book the company I'm selling for gave me when I spent a day in their training class." But that's not good enough. Would you really give your money to someone who hasn't read at least three books on the very topic they're selling you a product for? Anyone who's not knowledgeable about long-term care, but tries to tell you that their LTC insurance is best, is nothing more than a salesperson.

2. "The more you buy, the more I make."

People with different financial situations are buying the exact same amount of LTC insurance all the time, and it doesn't make sense. Talk to someone with $500,000 in assets and $70,000 of income, then to someone with $100,000 of assets and $20,000 of income, and both were probably sold the exact same amount of long-term care insurance.

Yet someone with $500,000 in assets and $70,000 of income shouldn't need the same amount of coverage as someone with $100,000 and $20,000 of income. That's because the person with more assets and income should be able to pay a little bit of their own long-term care without making much of a financial sacrifice. And if they can do that, shouldn't they be saving on their LTC insurance? Of course.

You probably don't have a zero deductible on your car insurance, right? And why? Because you can afford to pay a few hundred dollars out of pocket for an accident or repair, and it's worth it to save the money on your auto insurance. Well, your LTC insurance should be the same way.

But long-term care salespeople don't tell you this because they'd lose commission if you bought a lesser policy. If a long-term care salesperson admitted that you only needed $50 of coverage a day versus $100 or coverage, they'd only make half the commission. So if someone tries to sell you a policy without even looking at your assets, expenses, and tax return, you can bet they're a salesperson.

3. "I only recommend one company."

Imagine that you're a farmer and you need to buy a new automobile. You're looking for a truck to haul feed and tools that has four-wheel drive as well to get through the snow and mud of country roads.

But what if you walked into a car dealer that only sold one kind of European sports car? What if the car dealer showed you the car and said, "Well, it's got four wheels, a trunk, and steering wheel. It's what you need." You'd probably turn around and walk out as soon as you realized that there were no trucks in the showroom.

So then why is it okay when advisors only sell one particular product from a certain company? If someone tells you they only offer one type of long-term care policy from one company, would you buy it without shopping around? Hopefully not.

4. "Your premium will go up."

No one's going to mention that your long-term care premiums can go up unless you ask. And even then, they may suggest that it's possible, but wave your concerns off.

Remember that companies can and will increase your premiums in the future, and if you can't afford your premiums, you'll lose your coverage, which means you won't get your money back.

5. "The company's new at this."

Just like you wouldn't get in a taxi driven by a 16-year-old, you should avoid companies that are new to LTC insurance. Odds are companies that have never offered long-term care policies before have no idea how to set rates and manage them in the future. This means that new companies will have to change their rates and benefits as they learn from their mistakes, which translates into increased premiums for you down the road, as well as other headaches.

6. "What you don't know won't hurt you."

How many times have we all heard that? If someone's trying to sell you LTC insurance, but avoids explaining things by telling you, "It's a complicated issue," you should beware. When this happens, either the salesperson doesn't understand it themselves or the policy will obviously be a bad choice if they took the time to explain it. Either way, it's not a good sign. If they can't explain everything about the LTC insurance they're offering, go to someone who can. Make sure you understand a policy before you buy it.

7. "I can save you 15% to 30% on your premiums."

This is something you're not likely to hear. Even if you bought your LTC insurance years ago, you could still save 15% to 30% of your premiums. But few people will tell you this.

8. "Your premiums are deductible."

It's true, but only if you become so sick that you're spending 7.5% of your income on medical expenses. Of course, once that happens, you wouldn't be eligible for long-term care from any company. Besides, even if you were, you wouldn't have money to buy LTC insurance because every last cent would be spent on care itself.

9. "You can compare long-term care companies yourself."

This is something else you're not likely to hear. There's actually software available that allows you to compare LTC policies side-by-side, and you should do just that before you buy long-term care insurance.

10. "There are other ways to protect your assets without buying long-term care insurance."

This is also something you'll never hear from someone trying to sell you LTC insurance. Not everyone qualifies for long-term care insurance. But if you need coverage, there's a way to protect your assets without buying LTC insurance.

You should be shown how to do this, as well as other options to buying LTC insurance. But if the person selling you a policy doesn't mention these options, they're simply a salesperson and not an advisor.

Do I Have Other Options?

You do have a few options besides buying LTC insurance. Some senior investors can self-insure, specifically those who can afford to spend up to $500,000 on long-term care without leaving your spouse impoverished. Unfortunately, this holds true for a very small percentage of the population.

But there's another option available, and it lets you lock in your costs, so you'll never have to worry about your premiums going up. Better yet, there's a way to be covered without an annual premium, which also covers your long-term care expenses and lets you change your mind and cancel your coverage if necessary. This means that you could get your money back if you realize you'll never need long-term care, and if you die without using it, your beneficiaries will get your money back.

For instance, let's say Tom is a healthy 60-year-old, and he deposits $50,000 into a special account for long-term care. One of three things is going to happen to Tom: he's either going to live, die, or need long-term care. If Tom continues to remain healthy, his money earns up to 5% and is liquid. This means that Tom can change his mind if he wants to take all his money back. He may lose some of the interest he's earned if he changes his mind, but his principal is guaranteed. If Tom dies, his beneficiaries get $100,000 tax free, which is double what he put in. And if Tom needs long-term care, his $50,000 deposit turns into $200,000 of tax-free money for long-term care costs.

It's a great option because your rates cannot be raised. But there are two key factors you should know. First, you must be healthy when starting this plan. If you're already sick, you won't qualify. Also, there is no inflation rider on this plan, which means you could outgrow it. But even with those two facts, this is a great hedge for seniors who don't want to buy LTC insurance and can afford to pay some of their own way.

Another option we've already mentioned is the government plan for coverage: Medicaid. Medicaid is an entitlement program covered by Social Security. If you've paid into Social Security you may qualify for Medicaid. But as with everything involving our government, you have to understand the rules in order to receive your benefits.

Medicaid is the Cadillac of all policies and pays 100% of all nursing home costs including medications. However, you must meet the eligibility requirements. As with the example of Jim and Mary, you must already have used all your savings and investments for long-term care in order to qualify. Essentially, Medicaid covers you if you're broke.

So what can you do? Well, don't give up. If you can't afford long-term care insurance or your loved one is already in a long-term care facility, you're not completely out of luck. There are things you can do such as half-a-loaf planning or name-on-the-check rules. In fact, there are lots of things you can do to protect your assets that are left. But you need professional help.

You shouldn't seek an attorney to help you with this unless they're an elder care specialist, because very few attorneys understand the issues of long-term care. Instead, you should find a person who works only with the particular issue of long-term care.

Also, there's one investment that cannot be taken for medical assistance or Medicaid purposes. It's called a Medicaid-friendly annuity, and these are extremely specialized annuities. There are hundreds of annuities out there, but almost none of them have the specific language required to ensure that a long-term care stay will not require it to be spent. Also, the rules and regulations for these annuities vary from state to state. So if your annuity doesn't specifically say that, you don't have one.

Your advisor or financial consultant may tell you that you have a Medicaid-friendly annuity. But if they do, ask them to prove it by showing it to you in writing. If they can't prove it in writing, then that annuity's not protected – no matter what they tell you. And isn't it better to find out that your annuity's not protected before you need it? So remember, there are very few Medicaid-friendly annuities in existence, so make sure you sit down with a competent professional to discuss this option.

> If your annuity is not Medicaid-friendly, you can actually end up in a great deal of trouble.

In fact, if your annuity is not Medicaid-friendly you can actually end up in a great deal of trouble. Your principal would be gone and the government won't pay for your care, and that would put you between a rock and a hard place. So make sure you're working with a competent specialist.

Let's take a moment and look at how these annuities work.

Remember Mary and Jim? They had $300,000 in investments, but when Jim needed long-term care, Mary was forced to spend $274,753. She only ended up keeping $25,247 – just enough for a few home repairs and a new car.

Well, let's say that Jim and Mary had their $300,000 in a Medicaid-friendly annuity. If that were the case, Mary would be in control of her finances. She could choose to spend as much of the $300,000 as she wanted on Jim's long-term care, or she could elect to keep the whole $300,000. Mary would have peace of mind, because she could protect all $300,000, or as much as she wanted.

What If I Can't Get it?

Unfortunately, Jim and Mary's dilemma is typical of a lot of people. Most seniors don't have enough assets to self-insure, they have too many assets to qualify for Medicaid, and they can't afford LTC insurance or don't qualify for it because of their health. So what if you can't get LTC insurance and don't qualify for Medicaid?

One thing you can do is make yourself eligible for Medicaid without going broke paying for long-term care. It is possible to qualify for Medicaid in many states without becoming impoverished, and that's through an asset protection plan. An asset protection plan protects your financial assets from Medicaid-required spending, catastrophic illness, creditors, and qualifies an institutionalized individual for Medicaid immediately. In other words, if you're already in a nursing home and paying out of pocket for your care, you can still qualify for Medicaid immediately and protect your remaining assets.

But the government is currently trying to change this type of plan to keep people from taking advantage of it. So regardless of whether you currently need long-term care or not, get and remain informed. Remember the Navy and the stress test of the ship's chains. It's always better to plan before problems arise.

Best of all, this kind of planning is completely legal. This is not a loophole, but your right under state and federal laws as they're written right now. It's part of the rule book; you just have to know about it.

Now that you better understand why long-term care is so important, we'll look at legal planning in the next chapter.

CHAPTER 7

Legal Planning

Another way to protect your hard-earned money is through legal planning. And as with everything else we've discussed, there are areas of legal planning that you've probably already covered, such as inheritance and estates. But there's also a lot your advisor hasn't told you, such as why you need a medical directive and how to avoid probate without a trust. As you'll soon realize, no one's told you the whole truth about legal planning, no matter how much you think you know.

Why the Industry Doesn't Give You the Whole Truth

You may realize that probate is a way for people to get some of your money. And you may realize that there's two types of probate: the kind that you go through while you're alive and that which occurs when you die. But no matter which kind of probate you're familiar with, you'll be happy to know that no investment ever has to go through probate. Better yet, you don't need to set up an expensive trust to avoid probate. In fact, avoiding probate is as easy as correctly titling your stocks, bonds, mutual funds, CD's, and bank accounts. By making sure everything is correctly titled, nothing you own will go into any kind of probate.

Obviously, no one wants their assets to go through probate – not you, not me, not your friends, no one. It's no secret that probate is a four-letter word that should be avoided at all costs. But if that's true, shouldn't your advisor already know that you don't want your assets to go through probate? And if he or she knows it, why hasn't he or she addressed this issue with you?

Especially when avoiding probate is easy. If you go to your advisor and say, "I don't want my assets to go through probate," he or she's going to pull out a special form and have you fill it out. On the form, you'll have to indicate who you want your assets to go to, but once you fill it out and sign it, that's it. No legal headaches, no waiting, no setting up estates. It's done.

By the way, you can do the same thing at your bank. If you go to your banker and tell them you don't want your assets and accounts going through probate, they're going to do the exact same thing.

So let's look at that question again. Since you don't want your assets to go through probate, and your banker and broker know that no one wants their assets to go through probate, why hasn't something already been done? If these forms are so easy to fill out and don't cost anything, why hasn't your broker already told you about them?

It's a simple answer. They want to keep your money in their possession as long as possible. The average probate is two or three years, and many last longer than that. And while your money's in probate, it stays right in your bank and brokerage accounts. Therefore, even when you're gone, your advisor and bank continue to make money off your assets.

So if you haven't already done so, tell your advisor that you don't want your assets to go through probate. Better yet, take your assets to an advisor who knows and cares about your best interests. After all, why hasn't your current advisor told you about this already? Do they not know about this, or do they just not care?

Inheritance...Good or Bad Thing?

Like a lot of investors, many seniors lost their bearings during the Internet boom of the 1990's. But thanks to the recent downturn of the past few years, we've been brought back to our senses. Unlike the "get everything you can" attitude of the 1990's, you realize that you're no longer in the accumulation period of your life. Depending on your age and situation, you're either preserving your assets or spending them to enjoy yourself.

The truth is that the Greatest Generation is a generation of savers, and you should feel proud of yourself for all your hard work. But you also have one big problem: you've raised a generation of spenders. We've all heard how baby boomers spend, spend, spend, and have saved next to nothing for retirement. If you ask me, this sounds like a problem waiting to happen. And what does that mean? It's time for a stress test.

Have you ever noticed how some people suddenly treat their parents differently once they turn 65? Maybe it hasn't happened to you personally, but a lot of seniors have had to deal with adult children who think that turning 65 means you suddenly take a stupid pill when it comes to money and that you can't think for yourself.

It's pretty ridiculous, especially once you put things into perspective. For example, here's Debbie, a retired widow with her house paid in full, no debt, $300,000 in investments, and a nice $20,000 nest egg in her checking account (just in case). Debbie loves her son, Steve, so she loans him a few thousand dollars every year. Yet now Steve has started asking her about her financial matters, bullying her with his opinion, even when she didn't ask for it. Steve, of course, is a baby boomer with a $300,000 mortgage, $40,000 of car debt, $40,000 in his 401(k), $10,000 in credit card debt, and absolutely no savings. Steve just borrowed $5,000 from his mother last week, but now he insists he knows what's best for her money.

If you know anyone whose children treat them like this, be sure to give them some moral support, because they need it. Remind them which generation built this country and which is spending it away.

By the way, what's a seven-letter word for sound financial planning for children? Inherit.

It sound's like a great joke, but it's not. Ask your children what you should do with your money, and they'll tell you to spend it. And you'd better believe them, because if you don't spend your money – they will!

> **Ask you children what you should do with your money, and they'll tell you to spend it!**

You may have driven the same car for 15 years because it was still in good shape, but what will happen once your children inherit your money? They'll head down to the Lexus dealer and buy a brand new luxury car with leather interior. And you know that cruise around the world you and your spouse never took because it was just too expensive? Well, once you leave your children their inheritance, it's "Hello, Disney World!"

So if there's something you really want to do, but haven't done it because it's too expensive, do it anyway. Treat yourself. It's your money. You've worked hard to save it, so aren't you entitled to enjoy it?

We all know that you can't take it with you. And unless you use some of your savings to enjoy yourself, it's going to end up in one of three places: your children's bank account, the nursing home, or the government. And since you're responsible for the risks your take with your money, shouldn't you also be responsible for its rewards?

A client once told me that he wants the last check he writes to be to the undertaker. And he wants it to bounce. That's a great mentality to have.

Your Finances Consist of More Than Your Money

If you ask a bunch of people how they're doing financially, you'll get a wide range of answers. Some will tell you they're doing great, that they made a 15% return last year. Others will tell you they're doing lousy, that they lost 10% or 15% last year. But do returns have anything to do with how you're doing financially?

Returns are certainly important, but great returns alone don't mean that you're doing all right financially. That 15% return you made last year doesn't matter much if you gave a big chunk of it to Uncle Sam, spent all of it on long-term care, or if your return was eaten up by probate and estate tax costs. So while your returns are important, they amount to nothing if you don't take care of your affairs. If you leave everything in chaos, your surviving spouse will not only pay out all those returns you've bragged about, but more. And with all the stress involved in cleaning up investments and accounts, not to mention taxes and other problems, he or she will probably be pretty angry at you.

The old adage is true: the one who takes care of the money dies first. So begin your legal planning immediately, and explain everything to your spouse.

Financial Powers of Attorney

Conservatorship probate, which is when probate occurs while the person is still living, is more frustrating and difficult than going through probate at death. For example, let's say that John's finances end up in conservatorship probate. John, who is married to Elaine, has come down with Alzheimer's, is no longer mentally capable of taking care of himself and his wife, and is unable to function. Since John has lost his legal capacity to think and act for himself, he's unable to take care of their home. With John in a nursing home, Elaine wants to sell their house and move into a condominium which requires no maintenance from her.

But without John's signature, she's unable to sell the house. And because of his condition, John can't sign the necessary papers to sell the house, which means Elaine's stuck in a difficult situation.

This scenario can apply to anything. Homes, IRAs, stock accounts—anything with John's name on it would essentially be frozen.

What Elaine needs is a durable power of attorney, which is a legal document that allows someone else to act on your behalf should you become incapacitated or unable to function. If John had named Elaine as his power of attorney, she'd be able to take care of everything.

If you and your spouse don't have a power of attorney, getting one should be the first thing on your to-do list tomorrow. Because if you find yourself in a situation similar to Elaine and John's, you'll have to jump through a lot of hoops to get things taken care of. You'd have to be appointed conservator of your own spouse, which means hiring an attorney, paying several thousands of dollars, and going before the court and asking to be appointed as your spouse's conservator. Once that's done, the court system will be looking over your shoulder every time you make a decision to ensure you're spending your money appropriately.

Yet you can avoid all of this just by paying an attorney $50 or $100 to get a power of attorney done. But you can't get a power of attorney after you are incapacitated, so do it now. Remember the Navy stress test: fix things before they become problems.

Medical Powers of Attorney

But even if you have a financial power of attorney, that's not enough. You need to make sure you have a power of attorney for medical purposes. It's called a Quality of Life Directive, although it used to be called a living will. But unlike a living will, a Quality of Life Directive is much more comprehensive.

Quality of Life Directives actually tell your loved ones how you want to be taken care of medically when you can't tell them yourself. How much pain control would you want? Would you want to be taken off life support? What if you were in a coma?

These are all very difficult questions, but you need to take the time to answer them. Otherwise the decisions will be taken out of your hands.

Fortunately, Quality of Life Directives cover just about every possible scenario you'd need to consider. Best of all, you can get them free from a number of places: your doctor, your hospital, online, you can even get them from a qualified senior advisor.

But it's not enough just to have a Quality of Life Directive. You need to have it with you in the event of an emergency. In fact three out of four people who have a medical power of attorney don't have it with them when they show up at the hospital for care. That's because no one carries it around with them. Most of us understand just how important a Quality of Life Directive is, so we put it in a safety deposit box or somewhere secure for safekeeping.

After all, do you stick your Quality of Life Directive in your pocket when you drive to the store for a few things? Probably not.

Let's say you go outside one Sunday afternoon to play with your grandkids, and you begin to have chest pains. You're having a heart attack, so your son or daughter rushes you to the hospital.

When you arrive at the hospital, the first thing the staff will do is shove a clipboard in your face to sign. And what's on that clipboard? A piece of paper that makes the hospital your power of attorney, and by signing it, all the good work you've done has been eliminated. It's done to protect the hospital, not you, so you need to have your Quality of Life directive with you.

And since it's not convenient to carry around the actual form with you at all times, there's an alternative. You can get a laminated card for your wallet that gives the hospital a number to call to obtain your medical power of attorney electronically. EMTs and hospital staff are sure to find it, since they check the patient's wallet or purse for a driver's license, identification, and insurance cards. If you have this card with those things, they'll see it and be able to obtain your Quality of Life Directive.

In order to get one of these cards, your Quality of Life Directive must be electronically filed. If you don't have one, ask your financial advisor why not. If they say they can't get one, you'd better find someone who can. One day your life may depend on it!

> A Quality of Life Directive is the best gift you can give your loved ones.

A Quality of Life Directive is the best gift you can give your loved ones. It's hard to know what we want to do with our own bodies, but it's even harder to decide what to do with someone else's body. So get this done if you love your family!

Beneficiary Planning

Another thing that's extremely important is the correct designation of your beneficiaries. Throughout my years in the financial services business, I've found that almost 99% of all people have their beneficiaries incorrectly designated. When this happens, not only are grandchildren and family members accidentally disinherited, but families lose the hard-earned money you left them.

For example, let's look at Frank and his wife, Sarah. Frank and Sarah have three sons, and each son has a son of his own. In other words, Frank and Sarah have three sons and three grandsons.

If Frank dies, Sarah gets the couple's money. Easy enough, right? Then once Sarah dies, it goes to the sons and grandsons according to her wishes.

But what if one of their sons dies before either of them do? Who are the beneficiaries in that situation?

At first, it doesn't seem like much of a problem. Most seniors indicate that their inheritance should be split evenly between all their children, and that makes sense, as long as all your children outlive you. But if one of Frank and Sarah's sons die before they do, a grandson gets left out. By indicating that their money should be split evenly among their sons, half of Frank and Sarah's money would go to each living son. And in the process, they'd leave out the grandson who needed the money most – the one who lost his father.

And that's not the only scenario. Even if Frank and Sarah pre-pared for the death of one of their sons, other things could happen. For example, let's say that one of Frank and Sarah's sons died, but they set up their wills so that each surviving son gets one third of their money, and the grandson who lost his father gets a third.

Sounds great, unless family quarrels and divorce enter the picture. Suppose that one of Frank and Sarah's surviving sons divorces his wife after they've inherited Frank and Sarah's money. What happens if their daughter-in-law is given the money in the divorce, then runs off and marries a lazy jerk who gambles it all away? Now Frank and Sarah have not only disinherited their divorced son, but a third of their money as well.

You may think you're fine because you've thought all this out in your will. If so, good for you, but you're still at risk for these kinds of problems.

Why? Because not everything is covered by your will. In fact, the vast majority of most people's assets don't go through their wills. Things such as life insurance, IRAs, 401(k)s, and annuities do not go through wills, and if you're like most senior investors, where is the bulk of your money? In your life insurance, your IRA, your 401(k), and your annuities. So even if your will makes sure your grandchildren will get their college tuition paid thanks to you, it doesn't matter if the money is in your IRA.

Many seniors designate their beneficiaries as joint owners of their investments and accounts. This is a dangerous situation to be in, because their actions put your money at risk. Let's say that you and your daughter have joint ownership of all the stocks in your portfolio, and that she was just involved in a car accident. Your daughter's okay, but is sued by one of the other drivers involved. As part of the lawsuit, that individual could go after your portfolio simply because your daughter's name is listed as a co-owner.

And it's not always accidents and greed that causes these kinds of problems. I once knew a brother and sister who didn't have any other living relatives. The brother had $300,000 in investments, while the sister had $100,000. They intended to look out for each other, so they pooled their money into one joint account.

Sadly, the sister became ill and needed long-term care. And as we discussed earlier, Medicaid doesn't cover long-term care until you're broke. So not only did the sister have to spend her $100,000 on her long-term care, but her brother's money was used as well. By setting up a joint account with his sister, the brother's assets dwindled from $300,000 to just $3,000 – the amount Medicare allowed him to keep.

As you can see, in an effort to solve one problem, many people find they've created another. So you need to know the whole picture before you make any changes.

No one willingly disinherits family members they love, but it is possible for accidents like these to take your money away from the people you want to have it. So now is the time to stress test your beneficiary planning, because once you're gone, there's nothing you can do.

CHAPTER **8**

What the Financial Industry Doesn't Want You to Know

■ ■

"I am more concerned with the return of my principal, rather than the return on my principal."

— Will Rogers
Actor / Author / Philanthropist

■ ■

A s seniors, this is the attitude you need to have when it comes to your finances. Unlike pre-retirement investors, you don't have 20 or 30 years to get back any money you might lose.

We've already mentioned that you should be out of the accumulation period and into the preservation period, or better yet, the spending period of your life. But as you'll soon learn, the financial services industry doesn't look out for people who want to preserve their wealth. They're too busy trying to force people to accumulate more money.

History

It used to be that when people needed to invest their money, they went to their bank. Some of us used saving accounts. We could buy bonds and other types of low-risk investments from our banker. Of course, we can still do that, but things certainly have changed.

As you probably remember, there was a time in this country when you could walk into your local bank, say hello to the manager, and he'd offer you a cup of coffee and chat a while. Not any more. Today, banks are like musical chairs. The teller who was there last week is gone, the manager sits in an office with his or her door closed, and even the names of banks change on a regular basis as mergers and buyouts have caused local and regional banks to all but disappear.

And it's not just the banks themselves that have changed. Our whole notion of banks have changed, too. No longer do rates subtly change over a period of time. For example, look at Certificates of Deposit. They've certainly gone down in recent years, and at an alarming rate. Of course, they were quick to go down, but they've been slow to go back up.

And what about the Federal Deposit Insurance Corporation (FDIC)? Remember when they ran out of money in 1991? Unless you're an astute investor, maybe not. If this comes as a surprise to you, don't be too hard on yourself. After all, how could you have known that it happened when this story didn't even make the news.

At the time, the media was too busy covering the Savings and Loan bankruptcy to pay any attention to the FDIC. So while newspapers and television focused on thousands of Savings and Loans across the country running out of money, the FDIC itself was almost belly-up. But actually, it's a good thing the media never covered this story. Because if they had, the 1990's would've probably turned into a depression instead of the huge boom it became.

Of course, if the FDIC had become news in 1991, you would've headed down to your bank and taken every last dollar out of your accounts. A lot of people would have done that, but can you imagine the impact that kind of panic would've had on our country? Lines of people waiting to take everything out of their bank accounts all across the country? If that had happened, we would've had more than Savings and Loan problems; banks would've gone bankrupt as well.

Actually, most people would not have gotten their money back. That's because banks don't keep 100% of their funds on hand. Banks keep only $12.00 in their safes for every $100 they have on deposit. And what about the FDIC? They keep only $1.26 on hand for every $100. That's a whopping $13.26 backing up your $100. It's certainly not very much, but it's okay because our money is safe in the bank, right? It is as long as we continue to believe in them. Then again, 339 banks went under from 1991 to 2001.

This is not to suggest that you stop believing in the security and safety of banks. Banks are great places to hold your money, but you need to be aware of how they work and what you have.

As you already know, the stock market has become an attractive alternative to banks when it comes to saving and investing for the future, especially now that technology like the Internet has made it easier for everyday people to buy and sell stocks easily and cheaply. In the past 10 years, the stock market has become an almost national pastime of sorts. No longer is it just for the wealthy and money-conscious investors. So while many of us have moved away from banks and toward stocks as a way of preparing for the future, we're trading some of that safety we had for the possibility of a higher return on our investment.

Because of this, many investors want to know the average rate of return for the stock market. After all, we're told that the average return should justify our security in Wall Street and remind us that our money's safe, right?

But just what is the average rate of return for the stock market? Is it 10%? 5%? 20%?

Well, the truth is that all those numbers are correct, depending on the time period you're talking about. From 1976 to 1986 the average rate of return was 21%. From 1961 to 1971 it was 11%, and from 1964 to 1974 it was 4%. And over a 65-year period, the average rate of return was about 8-9%.

Is that 8-9% less than you expected? Does it make you nervous or less confident in the stock market? It shouldn't, because you shouldn't care about a 65-year period. After all, who retires for 65 years? No one! So how does that average rate of return impact you? It doesn't.

The Big Lie (Average Rate of Return)

The bottom line is that the average rate of return is the biggest lie you'll ever hear from the financial services industry. Every part of investing forces its average annual return on you, telling you it's a benchmark for comparison and the most important number you should be concerned with. That is simply not true.

Everyone in the financial services industry talks about how important the average rate of return is. Mutual funds use their average rate of return to convince you to buy their fund, brokers talk about the average rate of returns for their firm's products, and even money magazines talk about average rate of return when comparing investments. But relying on this is misleading, and here's why.

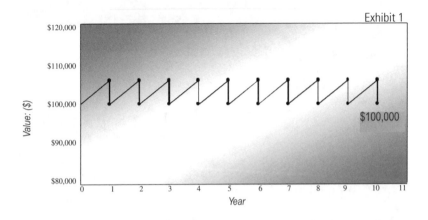

Exhibit 1

Let's say you own an investment that earns 6%. Now if you take 6% out of that investment, your balance in the account should remain consistent. In other words, if you have $100,000 in a CD earning 6%, it goes up to $106,000. If you take out 6% of that, you're back to $100,000. This continues year after year, and you make a consistent $6,000 without losing any money. (Exhibits 1 and 2)

Retirement Withdrawal (Assumptions) Deposit: $100,000				Exhibit 2
10 yr average return 6.0%			WIthdrawal rate per year 6.0%	
Year	Rate of Return	Beginning Value ($100,000)	Withdrawal	Ending Value
1	6.0%	$100,000	$6,000	$100,000
2	6.0%	$106,000	$6,000	$100,000
3	6.0%	$106,000	$6,000	$100,000
4	6.0%	$106,000	$6,000	$100,000
5	6.0%	$106,000	$6,000	$100,000
6	6.0%	$106,000	$6,000	$100,000
7	6.0%	$106,000	$6,000	$100,000
8	6.0%	$106,000	$6,000	$100,000
9	6.0%	$106,000	$6,000	$100,000
10	6.0%	$106,000	$6,000	$100,000

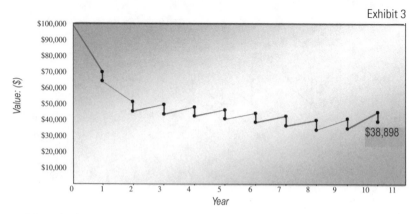

Exhibit 3

Now let's compare that to another investment that also has an average rate of return of 6%. Let's say you own $100,000 of a mutual fund, and it does the following: it loses 30% of it's value, then loses 20%, then makes 10%, makes another 10%, makes 10% again, makes another 10%, makes yet another 10%, makes 10% again, then makes 20%, and finally makes 30%. (Exhibits 3 and 4)

Monte Carlo — Assumptions			Exhibit 4
Deposit: $100,000			
10 yr average return 6.0%		Withdrawal rate per year 6.0%	
Example A			
Year	Rate of Return	Beginning Value ($100,000)	Withdrawal	Ending Value
1	-30.0%	$70,000	$6,000	$64,000
2	-20.0%	$51,200	$6,000	$45,200
3	10.0%	$49,720	$6,000	$43,720
4	10.0%	$48,092	$6,000	$42,092
5	10.0%	$46,301	$6,000	$40,301
6	10.0%	$44,331	$6,000	$38,331
7	10.0%	$42,164	$6,000	$36,164
8	10.0%	$39,781	$6,000	$33,781
9	20.0%	$40,537	$6,000	$34,537
10	30.0%	$44,898	$6,000	$38,898

With the mutual fund, your $100,000 fell to $70,000. Of course, if you took out $6,000, you're left with $64,000. The next month, that amount would fall to $51,000, and by taking out another $6,000, you're now left with $45,000. Of course, now you start making 10%, but it doesn't cover your recent withdrawals. That 10% doesn't make up the $6,000 you took out.

In fact, by the end of this time, you're left with less than $39,000 – even though you made 20% and 30% on the last two years. So despite that average rate of return of 6%, you've still lost money.

But what if it goes the opposite way? Let's say the fund makes 30%, then makes 20%, before making 10% six times in a row, losing 20%, then losing 30%. Then you'd have $105,000. It's a lot more damaging on the downside than it is beneficial on the upside. You'd lose more than 60% on the downside, but on the upside you're only gaining 5%. It's not much different from earning 6% in a CD. (Exhibit 5)

Monte Carlo — Assumptions				Exhibit 5
Deposit: $100,000				
10 yr average return 6.0%			Wlthdrawal rate per year 6.0%	
Example B				
Year	Rate of Return	Beginning Value ($100,000)	Withdrawal	Ending Value
1	30.0%	$130,000	$6,000	$124,000
2	20.0%	$148,800	$6,000	$142,800
3	10.0%	$157,080	$6,000	$151,080
4	10.0%	$166,188	$6,000	$160,188
5	10.0%	$176,207	$6,000	$170,207
6	10.0%	$187,227	$6,000	$181,227
7	10.0%	$199,350	$6,000	$193,350
8	10.0%	$212,685	$6,000	$206,685
9	-20.0%	$165,348	$6,000	$159,348
10	-30.0%	$111,544	$6,000	$105,544

Stocks are similar because they provide long-term real returns of 8-9%. Despite changes in stock prices over time, these 8-9% returns exist because of the rising earnings and dividends of corporations. In fact, the sum of real dividend yields and earnings growth during 1871-1997 was 6.7% once adjusted for inflation. So in other words, the long-term return on stocks is almost identical to the 8-9% return provided by the stock market itself.

Fundamental returns actually have most influence over the actual returns of stocks in the long-term. As you can see in Exhibit 6, the fundamental returns and market returns from 1872-1997 converge again and again, proving just how similar these two are.

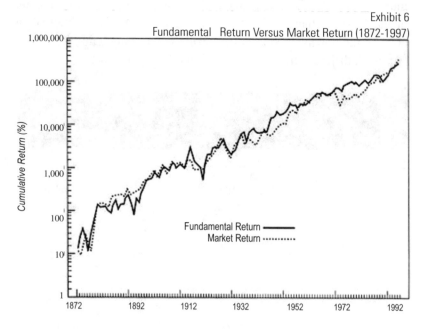

Exhibit 6
Fundamental Return Versus Market Return (1872-1997)

In comparison, both the CD and mutual fund had an annual rate of return of 6%, but you'd more than likely lose money with a fund or stocks. This is why the average rate of return is a big lie.

As a senior investor, you need to ask yourself the following: "Is my retirement controlling my investments, or are my investments controlling my retirement?"

Let me explain. If the stock market goes down 30% in one year, what would you do? Would you cut back and not spend any money? If you have a nice cruise planned to Alaska, but your nest egg is suddenly cut back by 30%, would you postpone your trip?

And what happens if someone gets sick the next year? Something happens to a family member? As we all know, any number of things can happen. Roofs start leaking, someone runs into your car, a flood ruins your basement. Next thing you know, you've delayed your trip for years.

But at this point in your life, should you really be delaying your trip? Of course not. If you want to go to Alaska, you should go and not let your investments control your retirement. This really hit home for me as I was recently watching a video shot two years ago of a class I conducted for 26 of my clients. Since then, four of them have passed away, and their average age was only 67.

So what's more important than the average rate of return? How you get it. You have to plan for the bear as well as the bull. So stress test your investments. If you can afford to make a withdrawal from your investments only when the market's doing well, you've got a problem. There's inevitably going to be a time when your investments are not going to be doing so well, and you need to be able to take money from your accounts then, too. And isn't it better to deal with this now than to find out you have a problem once something happens? Absolutely!

Rearview Investing

Another thing that a lot of investors do today is what's called rearview investing. We've all heard the saying that hindsight is

20/20, but some of us take it a little too literally when it comes to the stock market.

Rearview investing is when someone chases after mutual funds or other investments because they've done well over the last year or so. If someone says, "Well, this fund made 285% return last year, so I'm going to get into it and double my money," then they're chasing yesterday's news. And as you can imagine, it's not a good idea.

The recent bull/bear market cycle provides a clear example of how harmful an undisciplined, emotional approach to investing can be. Investors poured a record $309 billion into equity mutual funds at the top of the market in 2000, purchasing shares at the highest possible price, while also pulling a record $50 billion from bond funds right before they made their meteoric rise.

A few years later, the opposite happened. Investors put a record $140 billion into bond funds in 2002, buying these bonds when interest rates brought their prices to a 45-year high. And where did they get the money to do this? By pulling a record $27 billion out of equity funds at the bottom of the market, selling at the lowest possible price. In both situations, irrational behavior led investors to do the exact opposite of what they should have done in both instances.

The Effects of Irrational Investing			
Year	Stock Funds	Bond Funds	S&P 500
2000	$309 billion	(-$50 billion)	1,509 – Market High
2002	(-$27 billion)	$140 billion	776 – Market

Source: Barra.com "Mutual Fund Facts and Figures," Investment Company Institute, 2003

So never use an investment's past performance as justification to get in and make money. And whatever you do, don't chase the market because you think you can land big returns in the process. A lot of investors have learned that doing so means you'll always be a day late and a dollar short – literally!

Do They REALLY Have Your Best Interest at Heart?

It's no surprise that a lot of investors work with investment management consultants, and although most of these consultants call themselves advisors, the title seldom fits.

By far the vast majority of "advisors" have a three-step financial plan:

- **Step One**: How much money do you have?

- **Step Two**: Where do you have it?

- **Step Three**: Let's move it here.

These financial advisors spend a lot of time trying to convince you why you need to move your money. They bring up products, stocks, and most importantly, average rate of return.

These brokers and salespeople are only interested in two things: how much money you're going make (because a happy client is a good client) and how much money he or she is going to make. Therefore, make sure your advisor's priority is how much you make, not how much he or she makes.

In recent years, the financial services industry has caught a lot of heat for bad and misleading practices. Arthur Levitt, the former head of the Securities and Exchange Commission (SEC), once said that "brokers are paid to buy and sell – not necessarily to look out for investors' best interests." Levitt also added that branch managers are part of the problem, because their compensation is based on production. He also said that the majority of brokers are not sufficiently trained to handle the wide variety of investment products they sell.

Remember the *Consumer Reports* story where the secret shopper who went to five brokers? After going to two independent advisors and three big name brokerage houses, the secret shopper reported that the independents did a better job. And as you might expect, independent brokers don't have a branch manager. So you can begin to see why the independents were better.

And investors have become understandably angry as they've learned the truth about Wall Street racketeering. Critics say during the bull market analysts and their firms had a powerful incentive to issue overly optimistic reports about many of the stocks they covered. In many cases, these firms had already collected huge fees by selling the companies' stock to the public and stood to collect even more in fees if the price of the stock remained high.

We've already learned that unbiased recommendations were a myth in the late 1990's. And even today, how many buy recommendations do you hear about and see versus sell recommendations? It's still pretty lopsided.

So while firms and analysts profited handsomely from these fees, investors who followed the advice of their firm's analysts fared poorly. A lot of senior investors fared poorly over the last few years because of their broker's advice, and that probably applies to you as well.

And now that you realize all of this, it's in your best interest to look for someone who is the opposite of these brokers and salespeople. The good will take care of itself, so be more concerned with the possible downside to your investments. This may sound pessimistic, but you need to look at the worst case scenarios that may arise in your life. Because if you're prepared to deal with your worst case scenario, anything else will be a welcome part of your life.

But how do most brokers and salespeople address the downside? Not surprisingly, most don't. Here's how the majority of seniors were informed about the potential downside to their investments:

Brokers would spend as much as several one-hour sessions telling the senior how great the particular investment is and how much money they stand to make from it. Once they had suffi ciently explained the product and gotten the investor excited, they simply mentioned a quick caveat that reminded them that noth- ing was guaranteed. Usually it's something like, "Now there's no guarantee about this, but if the market goes down and you hold it long enough, it should take care of itself."

That's it. Those two sentences are how the majority of brokers in this country address the downside of any investment. If that's the best they can say, do you really think they have your best interests at heart?

At this point in your life, you already have a comfortable retire- ment. Why risk it all by ignoring the worse case scenario that could happen to you? Most of us believe in Murphy's Law, and many of us count on the worse case scenario. I want to be prepared for the worst thing that can happen to me and my family, because if I can live with that, everything else will take care of itself – and your investments should be handled the same way.

As an investor, you should be looking for an advisor who is willing to tell you in detail the worst that could happen. If an advisor says to you, "Here's the worst thing that could happen. Can you live with that?" then you've found a professional who truly has your best interests at heart.

Slow and Steady Wins the Race

When does –30 + 43 = 0? When you're looking at the return of your investments, that's when. If you own an investment that loses 30% of its value, you'll need to make 43% the following year just to break even. In fact, if you have $100 and lose 50%, you've got $50, right? Well, in order to get back your original $100, you'd have to make 100%, or double your money, the following year.

How does a Loss Affect Seniors?

According to a recent study by AARP, 77% of individuals between the ages of 50 and 70 who own stock indicate that they lost money in either individual stocks, mutual funds, or other investment accounts during 2002-2003. Worse yet, the majority of those individuals were forced to make lifestyle changes due to their investment losses.

Adjustments Made to Lifestyle Due to Losses	Percentage of Those Who Lost Money
Budget money more carefully	59%
Reduced spending	42%
Took fewer vacations	34%
Postponed a major purchase	30%
Had difficulty paying for health-care or prescription drugs	9%

So you can see that when you take a hit, it takes an awful lot of effort just to get back to where you started. Worse yet, this doesn't even mention the loss of time involved. When something like this happens, you also lose the time value of money, which is also costing you. And no one wants to take unnecessary risks.

Let's say that I'm going to race you for a comfortable retirement, and I have two cars for us. Since I'm such a nice guy, I'm going to allow you to choose which car you want to drive, and I'll use the other one. The first car has seat belts, reinforced doors, a fire extinguisher, and air bags, but can only go 80 mph. The other car has no safety equipment, is made with lots of plastic, is very light, and can go 140 mph.

So you can choose a slower car that will not only withstand an 80 mph crash into a brick wall, but you'll be able to walk away. Or you can choose a faster car that will zip along at 140 mph, but may easily flip and will rip apart like paper if you have an accident. Which do you want to drive?

The slower car, of course! But yet, you're more likely to win with the faster car. Why would anyone choose a car they know is slower in this situation? Because it's safe.

Now, what if you could participate in stocks without any market risk. There's a particular technique that works a lot like the crash-proof car. It gets you where you want to be, but you can't crash and get hurt. It's a new hybrid technique that's been around for just over 10 years, and it's perfect for people who don't want to take any risk but still want stock market-like returns. It's a great option for every senior investor in the country.

These hybrids tie your return to stock market indices such as the S&P 500, Dow Jones, or the Nasdaq 100, and guarantee your principal against market loss. In other words, you won't lose your money if the market goes down.

Basically, you choose an index to follow, and you earn interest that is tied to that index. These investments don't rise as fast as the stock market, so if you chose the Nasdaq 100 as your index, and it goes up 20, you might make 15, but if the index drops you walk away unscathed. These hybrids automatically buy low and sell high, which means they make money during the good times, but you take no losses during the bad times.

For example, from 1964 to 1974, the NYSE had the annual results shown in Exhibit 7. If you had an account with $100,000 in 1964, you would have ended up with just under $92,000 in 1974. In other words, you would have lost $8,000 over a decade.

Exhibit 7

1964	1965	1966	1967	1968	1969	1970	1971	1972	1973	1974
13.0%	9.1%	-13.1%	20.1%	7.7%	-11.4%	0.0%	10.8%	15.6%	-17.4%	-29.7%

By comparison, a hybrid would have gone up when the market went up, but you wouldn't have lost any money when the market dipped. By using a hybrid investment, you would have made $194,000 instead of $92,000 – a difference of $102,00.

Of course, there's no such thing as a perfect investment. If there was, I'd be sitting on my yacht in the Caribbean rather than

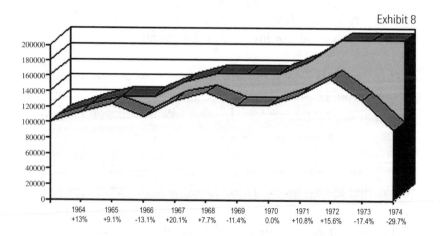

Exhibit 8

writing this book. But it could be a good fit for you to preserve your wealth. So ask your advisor about these hybrids and make sure you understand the differences between these and other investments before you make a decision. But no matter what, you should know about them so you can make an informed choice about what's best for you.

How's your investment doing? It depends.

A few years ago, before the market started doing badly, a lot of people were happy with their mutual funds. People would come and tell me very proudly, "My mutual fund made 14% last year!"

I would respond by apologizing to them and telling them how sorry I was. Naturally, these people would say, "What do you mean you're sorry?" and I would explain that their fund might have made 14%, but that the market made 28%.

"You only made half of what the market did," I'd say. Of course, sometimes people would come up and tell me they lost 3% of their portfolio. They'd look miserable, and become confused when I congratulated them. "You should feel good," I'd say, "the market's down 15%. You're doing great by comparison!"

Sadly, most people don't have

> ## Buy and Hold ... Really?
>
> If you invested $10 from 1928 to 2002, how much would you have?
>
> If you used a buy & hold strategy–$10,957
>
> If you missed the 30 best months of the market–$154
>
> If you missed the 30 worst months of the market–$1,317,803
>
> If you missed both the 30 best and 30 worst months–$18,558

an adequate yardstick against which to measure their investments. And without something to compare your investments to, you're liable to get panicked and make rash decisions when it comes to your money. Not only is the grass always greener on the other side, but the money seems to be, too.

For example, think of a river. If you live in a river town and the news reports that the river level is at 28 feet, how do you know if that is good or bad? You wouldn't know unless you also knew what the flood level is. Without it, 28 feet is just a number.

If the flood level is 35 feet, then everything's fine. But if the flood level is 25 feet, then it might be time to head to higher ground.

Investments are the same way. Without a proper measuring stick, your returns are just numbers. So if you're not already measuring all your investments against an appropriate measuring stick, you need to begin to do so immediately.

And as we've discussed before, you need to be testing your investments. Besides the Navy's stress test of pulling on chain links, another way of doing this is by giving your investments the tea bag test. In other words, you put your portfolio into some hot water and see how it performs.

Over the last decade, people have been so misled by high rates of return that they forgot some basic principles of investing. You may like roller coasters, but stay away from funds and investments that go up and down like an elevator. Investing is like the story of the tortoise and the hare – slow and steady wins the race.

CHAPTER 9

What Is It You Want Your Portfolio To Do?

hroughout this book, we've discussed a lot of options you and other senior investors can use to improve your financial situation. But before you begin putting these different ideas into action, you should take a few moments to prepare and decide how to best take advantage of your new knowledge.

As we've explained in previous chapters, each of the suggestions and investments mentioned may or may not be appropriate for you. It's up to you to determine what will benefit you and what won't. Just as you should do a stress test of your current investments, you should also test out any changes to your portfolio before you actually make them.

What Should Your Financial Plan Look Like?

The previous chapter explained that your financial situation is completely different from that of your children. And likewise, your financial needs may differ from your friends' and other seniors. For example, a couple who continues to make a mortgage and car payment each month will need a different level of income than a couple whose home and cars are already paid for. An even better example is an individual who must pay for their spouse's long-term care costs, because the amount of income needed for these expenses is vastly greater than for an individual or couple who are in good health.

We all have different priorities, and your financial plan should reflect your own. Unfortunately, most brokers and financial advisors use a cookie cutter, "one size fits all" approach. But rather than continuing to hold and invest in funds and investments that someone convinced you that you needed, you should begin evaluating things for yourself and determining what you really need to be doing with your investments.

Analyze Your Goals

The first step to changing your financial plan is analyzing your goals, since they will be the driving force behind everything you'll do. Most investors set goals for themselves when they first start out investing, but never update them to reflect the changes in their lives.

Worse yet, others simply start investing without any goals at all. At most, these individuals simply want to "make money." Yet making money isn't the goal of investing; making money is how you achieve your goals and dreams. Your goal may be to buy a second home in Florida and afford to travel back and forth between your houses each year, but making money on your investments is how you do that. So your goals aren't about money, but what you'll do with it.

Now is the time to analyze your goals. If they're old and out-of-date, then you need to change them to reflect your current financial needs and wants. If you don't have any to begin with, start from scratch and decide what you want from your investments.

Are you looking to reduce taxes on your Social Security income? If so, you're going to take advantage of different investments than someone who wants to make sure they don't accidentally disinherit their grandchildren. A review of your portfolio and taxes may tell you that you're paying a lot of taxes on money you're not spending. In that situation, your needs are completely different from someone who needs to make sure they can afford long-term care.

Analyze Your Portfolio

Once you've addressed your goals, it's time to look at your portfolio. Be sure to stress test each investment you own, as well as your overall holdings to see where you are at risk.

As you go through this step, see if you're covered for just about anything that might happen. Remember the worst case scenario: you should pose all sorts of combinations and problems to see what could happen. In other words, don't just see what would happen if you or your spouse spent a week in the hospital, see what would happen if one of you needed long-term care and needed to replace the roof on your house at the same time.

Also, remember to ignore the rate of return of your investments as you make these comparisons. You've already learned how this is not only misleading, but a big lie. So instead of saying, "Oh, this makes an average return of 12%. We're fine," compare your investments to an appropriate benchmark.

Using a proper benchmark is the key to making any improvement to your investments. Doing a financial stress test means not just looking at investments, but reviewing your tax return every year, having your accounts and beneficiaries reviewed for correct titling and designation, and reviewing your legal affairs annually. All this may seem like a lot of work and headache, but if you don't do it, your financial plan will go right down the tubes.

If you go to the doctor with a headache, he doesn't give you an aspirin and send you home. He gives you a series of tests to see what the problem could be. It could be a tumor, an aneurysm, or a stroke, but the only way of knowing is by conducting tests. Your finances should be handled the same way.

In fact, if a doctor sent you home with aspirin and you had a stroke, what would happen to that doctor? He'd lose his license. So if your advisor tries to tell you everything's fine and pushes you out the door, it's time to find a new advisor.

Do They Match?

Once you've gone through both your goals and your current portfolio, it's time to see how well they match. If you've done a good job stress testing your investments, you've probably found a few surprises that you want to fix. If so, don't be upset. After all, better to find out now than once it becomes a problem.

For example, you may learn that your mutual funds are geared toward accumulating wealth, and you've been losing some money over the past couple of years. This does not help you achieve your goal of paying for your grandchildren's college education. In order to achieve this, you need to be preserving what you have, not risking it to get more.

Likewise, you may have learned that you're paying a lot of taxes on money you're not spending. Of course, if you didn't know you were giving all that extra money to Uncle Sam to begin with, your investments certainly weren't going to minimize your taxes for you.

This will help you realize how your goals and investments can work together to give you peace of mind – and keep the money you've worked so hard to earn!

But now that you've found some of these problems with your portfolio and realized that they don't match your goals, you have to ask yourself, "Why didn't my advisor already tell me this?" For many people, the vast difference between their goals and the investments they hold lets them know that they need a new advisor – one that will put their needs first. Are you one of those people?

What Can You Do to Make Them Work Together?

The answer is a lot. First, you need to decide whether or not to change advisors. Only you know the answer to that, but at this point, you should have a strong idea whether your advisor has simply missed a few things or cares more about lining his or her own pockets than looking out for you.

The things you've learned from this book should be a pretty good indicator. In fact, the more you've learned, the more you probably realize that there's a lot your advisor doesn't know. But if you've already heard everything in this book from your advisor, give yourself a pat on the back. Because if so, you're getting your money's worth, no matter what he or she is charging.

Next, you can act on the investments and ideas you've learned about. Talk to your advisor about the things in this book that most interest you, and get more information about other options that will help you achieve your goals. Don't feel that you have to do it all in one sitting, but begin by fixing the biggest problem with your portfolio or the one that bothers you the most.

The topics discussed in this book can literally save you thousands of dollars. Even if you act on just two or three of the investments and ideas mentioned, they could be worth anywhere from $1,000 to over $300,000 over time. And once you start making these changes, you'll see the improvements they can make. Eventually, you'll wonder why you hadn't done this years ago.

Can you have your cake and eat it too?

Absolutely. In fact, by reading this book you've already learned how to do it.

If you ask seniors who have used the information in this book how their portfolio is doing, they will almost always tell you that they have all their financial affairs in order. And that's the best answer anyone can give.

Seniors who have learned these things are not paying unnecessary taxes on their Social Security income, or at risk of accidentally disinheriting their grandchildren, or paying taxes on money they are not spending. They have peace of mind and are keeping their hard-earned money. Isn't that the real goal of retirement?

I wish you good luck and a wonderful retirement!